D1238822

The Resilience Formula

LEARNING
OPPORTUNITY
AHEAD

The Resilience Formula

A GUIDE TO

PROACTIVE NOT REACTIVE PARENTING

Donna M. Volpitta, Ed.D.
Joel D. Haber, Ph.D. "The Bully Coach"

N.W. Widener Publishers

NEW YORK

Editorial Production: BookCrafters, LLC; Jennifer Bale-O'Connell

Book design: Lori S. Malkin

PHOTOGRAPHY/ILLUSTRATION CREDITS:

Front cover illustration: © Lightspring

Back cover photographs: *(top)* Sandra P. More; *(middle)* Mike Stoner; *(bottom, clockwise from left)* Donna Volpitta; Michel Lujan; Pedro Simao, sxc; Lori Ehrlich, © Joshua Hodge Photography, iStockphoto.

Page 55: © Tool Kits for Kids LLC, All rights reserved.

Page 59, photographs: *(top)* © David Coleman | Dreamstime.com; *(left)* © Kalvis Kalsers | Dreamstime.com; *(bottom)* © Barbara Helgason | Dreamstime.com;

ISBN 978-0-9852365-0-2 (paperback)

Printed in the United States of America

To Ginger, my mother and mentor;
Richard, my husband and partner;
and Marco, Jenna, Sarah and Stefan,
my guinea pigs and inspiration.
I love you all more than I could ever say.
—DMV

———◆◆◆———

To Evelyn, my mother,
for her unending support and resilience;
Cindy, Alyssa, Scott, family and friends who
continue to bring much happiness and smiles to
my life—with much love and gratitude!
—JDH

Table of Contents

Acknowledgements

Thanks to all of the people—more than can be named—who helped us to make this book possible. We know that a big part of resilience is support, and we are incredibly lucky to have so much of it!

From Reactive to Proactive

Last week a mom called us with some urgent news: her family was in crisis.

Her son, Eric, a typical teenager, had been trying to balance all of the demands of middle school, social pressure, and family dynamics. Not unlike many of his peers, Eric struggled with keeping everything together, and when things got particularly tough, Eric used music as an outlet. Eric's prized possession was his iPod, on which he stored all of his favorite tunes.

This is what happened: the previous evening, Eric's parents had gone out for a bit, leaving him with his younger sister and brother. In the middle of dinner, they got a call. Apparently Eric's iPod had fallen in the toilet, and the loss had caused their eldest child to lose control. When his parents arrived home, they discovered a path of destruction. Eric had stormed about, breaking things throughout the house.

His parents reacted strongly to the sight of the wreckage. They got angry, and started yelling. A screaming match ensued, and, in the middle of it all, Eric fled out the door. He left his home at 11 p.m. in bare feet, in twenty-degree weather.

Eric's parents had assumed that he would come right back, but they were wrong. It was a half an hour before they got a call from Eric's aunt. She told them that Eric had called and asked her to pick him up at a shopping center located two and a half miles from his house.

When a preschooler is testing boundaries, it is frustrating to parents. *When a teenager is testing those boundaries, it can be dangerous to his or her survival.* Luckily, in Eric's case, it did not turn out tragically. But it could have. And if his parents don't teach him effective coping strategies, the next time it could.

From the Mundane . . . to the Dangerous

When our children make us angry, our emotions often run high. For both ourselves and our children, anger fuels more anger, and the need for control often leads to a deadlock—not a great combination if we want to get past the moment without hurt feelings.

The patterns of parenting that we set early on in a child's life can have a significant effect on how that child will deal with situations—from the mundane to the dangerous—in the future.

But here's the thing that most parents don't think about: *the patterns of parenting that we set early on in a child's life can have a significant effect on how that child will deal with situations—from the mundane to the dangerous—in the future.*

Yes, through our everyday interactions, we are preparing our child to face peer pressure, bullies, potential predators, and the unfortunate tragedies that can come calling in their lives. Really, what we are doing is *training a child in resilience*. **Resilience** helps in determining how people handle challenging situations: *will they get overwhelmed and give up, or will they find a way to succeed?* In the example just cited, Eric was faced with a challenge—and the reality was, he didn't know how to cope.

What Has Shaped the Teacup Generation?

Generation Y is being referred to as the "teacup generation." Why? *Because these kids are so fragile that as soon as something goes wrong, they shatter like teacups!* It is the generation that has been raised by "helicopter parents," parents that wanted so badly for their children to be happy that they have consistently swooped in to save them from even the slightest inconveniences. It is a generation that has not had to delay gratification because as soon as they have had to wait for anything, their parents have handed them the iPod, the iPhone, or another form of electronic entertainment. It is a generation that has been coached and guided through every bump in the road, leaving them helpless to fend for themselves.

It is also a generation that is growing up in a world that is changing quickly. The technological advances available to this generation are like none that we have seen before. Young people are often being exposed to situations that they are not prepared to handle, and the consequences can be significant. A recent survey of parents in the U.S. showed that *53 percent of parents with eleven-year-olds said their child is part of a mainstream, **adult-intended** social network.* Ours is an era of sexting and cyberbullying, a time in which pedophiles are able to find their prey in the comfort of their living rooms. Thus,

11

the teacup generation is a generation that needs to learn how to make resilient decisions.

The Beauty of Being a Proactive Parent

In this book, we teach **proactive parenting**—*parenting in a way that actively considers how to teach resilience to children through everyday challenges.*

There are so many parenting books available that tell us what makes a good parent. We know that authoritative parenting styles tend to result in children that are happy, capable and successful.* These parents have high demands and establish rules for their children, but they encourage their children to have a say in how those rules are established and maintained. They listen to what their children say and respect their opinions. They explain the decisions that they make. Their discipline methods are not punitive, but supportive. They are consistent and predictable in their expectations and responses.

It is not easy, however, to find information about HOW to be that type of parent, particularly when emotions and control battles come into play. This is what we set out to do.

Proactive parenting puts *you* in control and helps you to make decisions that benefit your children over the long term. While no one is going to be the "perfect" proactive parent, there is a formula you can use—with specific tools and strategies to follow to build resilience in your child through his or her everyday challenges.

---

*http://psychology.about.com/od/developmentalpsychology/a/parenting-style.htm

In this book, we first outline **a framework** for proactive parenting. The framework offers four key concepts that parents can teach to help kids face challenges successfully. Those four concepts are what we call the *Four Ss*: self, situation, strategies, and support. We use these four concepts to guide the lessons that we are to use in daily interactions with our children, as they inform how we evaluate and act in response to challenge.

> *We teach proactive parenting—parenting in a way that actively considers how to teach resilience to children through everyday challenges.*

Then, we offer **a tool** that all parents can use to effectively convey those concepts. The tool is what we call, *"scripting."* Triggerscripts, the first type of script, trigger, or activate, an escape from a situation until all parties involved are ready to think logically. Once everyone is calm, parents use scripting as their tool to teach a child how to handle challenges effectively.

Finally, we put it all together in **a plan**—one that recognizes that we all are emotional beings, especially when it comes to interacting with our loved ones. The plan prepares us to be able to effectively use the scripting tools to teach the Four Ss in everyday interactions with our children now and in the future. Therefore, this plan instructs us in *proactive parenting*.

Can You Be a Proactive Parent?

The first, and hardest question to ask yourself is, *Can I be open to a new way of thinking about parenting?* If you answer in the affirmative, then *this book is for you.* The strategies are not hard, but they do take a shift in thinking—a change in the way you look at common, everyday interactions.

Proactive parenting takes consistency. It requires persistence. It necessitates a change in the way that you think about parenting. It is not an easy fix, but it is a long-term solution. It takes a commitment, but it offers immense payback.

If you are ready, let's begin the journey.

PART ONE

The Goal: Resilience

Chapter One

◆◆◆

Why Resilience?

Chris Waddell was a promising young skier back in 1988 when he was a freshman at Middlebury College. Good looking and popular, he had everything going for him. But on the first day of Christmas vacation that year, Chris went skiing, and his ski popped off. The ensuing accident left him paralyzed from the waist down.

How did Chris handle this tough and totally unexpected challenge, something that might overwhelm most people?

With determination and resolve! Chris was determined to get back on the slopes, and it was only about a year later that he began skiing on a mono-ski. A little more than two years later, Chris was named to the U.S. Disabled Ski Team.

Chris went on to become the most decorated male skier in the history of the Paralympic Games, winning twelve medals over four games and spending a total of eleven years on the U.S. Disabled Ski Team.

To top it off, Chris became the first paraplegic to summit Mt. Kilimanjaro, an event that was documented in an award-winning film, *One Revolution*. What is Chris doing today? He is touring and lecturing with the film and Nametags, his student outreach educational program about resilience. His motto? "It's not what happens to you; it's what you do with what happens to you."

How was Chris able to do all that he did? Why did he not quit when he had a traumatic accident that might sink many people?

Chris attributes his resilience to his parents' parenting style. He says that when he was young, his parents *let him experience failure, but also supported him through it.* He loves to tell the story of his experiences skiing on a ski team: for a year and a half, he never finished a race. Many times he came home wanting to quit, *but his parents helped him get back out there and try again.* So when he had the accident that left him a paraplegic, quitting was not an option.

> Resilience is something that parents can teach every day.

Is this kind of resilience something that all of us parents can teach to our kids? The answer is, "Yes!" In fact, *resilience is something that parents can teach every day through the way that they interact with their children in the face of any type of challenge.*

A Positive Coping Response

Traditionally, **resilience** has been defined as *the ability to respond positively to adverse situations, typically those that arise to such proportions as natural disasters, war, or crippling accidents.* When faced with these kinds of situations, some people are emotionally destroyed, while others thrive. Those who thrive are "resilient."

Recently, resilience has been considered in a broader sense, *encompassing a person's ability to cope with any stress or adversity.*

How does a person cope when he loses a job, breaks a bone, or even gets into a car accident? Some people handle these situations better than others and are able to "bounce back" quickly. This is resilience.

The more we learn about resilience, the more we realize that it is a *process* rather than an innate characteristic. As we live our lives every day, we learn coping strategies. These coping strategies make up our resilience when facing adversity or challenges. Resilience is built through the quality of our everyday interactions, producing a "steeling effect" (Rutter, 2006) in us.

Planting Seeds for a Resilient Character

Our goal is to give parents specific strategies for how to take challenging moments and turn them into opportunities to teach resilience. Most parenting books that are currently available provide parents with overarching guidelines for the qualities they should instill to build resilience. Let's take a quick look at those qualities.

In his book, *Building Resilience in Children and Teens,* Kenneth R. Ginsburg outlines the 7 C's model of resilience. This model provides a plan to help parents make decisions about how to raise resilient children. Ginsburg outlines seven integral, interrelated components that form a resilient character:

1- COMPETENCE: When parents notice what young people are doing right and give them opportunities to develop important skills, it builds a feeling of competence. If parents don't allow young people to recover by themselves after a fall, it undermines their sense of competence.

2- CONFIDENCE: Young people need confidence to be able to navigate the world, think outside the box, and recover from challenges.

3- CONNECTION: Connections with other people within schools and communities offer young people security; this allows them to stand on their own and develop creative solutions.

4- CHARACTER: Young people need a clear sense of right and wrong and a commitment to integrity.

5- CONTRIBUTION: Young people who contribute to the well-being of others receive gratitude and learn that contributing feels good. As a result, these young people may more easily turn to others for assistance in the future, doing so without shame.

6- COPING: Young people who possess a variety of healthy coping strategies are less likely to turn to dangerous quick fixes such as alcohol when stressed.

7- CONTROL: Young people who understand that privileges and respect are earned through demonstrating responsibility learn to make wise choices and feel a sense of control.

These seven categories provide the seeds for developing resilience and are part of a total approach to "blanket" your child with protection. Ginsburg's book provides a great framework for parents to think about how to approach parenting from a "resilience" perspective.

For example:

◆ COMPETENCE: Should I sign my child up to be in a soccer program? Should I encourage him or her to audition for the play or take art classes?

◆ CONFIDENCE: Should I wait before I offer to help my child on the monkey bars? Should I criticize the mistake he or she made or let it go? Should I gush over the sub-par piece of art my child made?

◆ CONNECTION: Should we go to religious services? Should we join the neighborhood association? Do I set up playdates for my child with kids from the neighborhood?

Ginsburg's 7 C's model of resilience:

1- Competence

2- Confidence

3- Connection

4- Character

5- Contribution

6- Coping

7- Control

◆ CHARACTER: Do I tell my kids to lie about their age to get a cheaper admission price at the museum? Do I encourage my children to stick up for others or stay out of conflict?

◆ CONTRIBUTION: Does my family actively engage in helping others? Should I take my kids to the nursing home to brighten someone's day?

◆ COPING: Do I give my child unstructured time to figure out what he or she likes to do in their leisure time? Do I help my child figure out how to structure their time to be able to finish their work?

◆ CONTROL: Do I actively teach my kids that there are some things you can control and some things you can't? Do I hand my child an electronic device every time he or she experiences the need to wait or do I teach him or her strategies to develop patience?

By actively considering the 7Cs when they make parenting *decisions,* parents can provide their children with an environment that fosters resilience.

Bringing it Home, Every Day, in a Practical Way

The tricky part here is that understanding such concepts is only a part of the puzzle! A harder part is *knowing how to take concepts with which we intellectually agree* **and apply or deliver them in everyday life as often as we should when faced with challenges that make us emotional.** Our human nature often gets in the way of delivering messages in a clear, consistent, and objective way.

Isn't it true that when we are exhausted, we sometimes cave? When we are stressed, we sometimes readily agree to something we normally would not? When faced with challenge, we typically react emotionally . . . and impulsively?

While Ginsburg's book provides an overall framework for resilient parenting, our book offers a practical plan for how to respond to everyday challenges. In times of challenge, our natural reactions as parents are counterproductive to fostering resilience. It is these critical times that we need the most help.

Challenge involves the parts of human nature that don't necessarily allow us to deliver these messages in the way that we would like. It is about *emotion.* It is about *stress.* It is about *exhaustion.* It is about *nervousness.* Thus, this book, *The Resilience Formula,* offers the strategies and techniques for building resilience *through life's challenging moments and using it not only to resolve the situation at hand, but also for obstacles that arrive in our future!*

Handling Challenges as Teachable Moments

Everyone, at every age, faces challenge almost every minute of the day. Here are some examples of ordinary challenges that face people of varying ages:

- a toddler trying to learn to climb a ladder at the playground;

- a preschooler learning to ride a bike;

- an elementary school student learning how to participate in, and complete, a group project;

- a middle school student trying to plan a school dance;

- a high school student making a decision as to whether to get in the car with a friend who has been drinking;

- a parent juggling the demands of dinner, homework, and a screaming toddler.

These are all challenges. How individuals handle the challenge(s) before them is based partly on the coping strategies they have learned from facing other challenges in the past. Therefore, as parents, we need to view each life challenge that faces our child *as a teachable moment.*

Growing The Seeds of Resilience

In this book, we talk about resilience as *our response to challenge.* We choose the word "challenge" because it is a broader term for everyday life events and does not just involve those that are especially adverse. This is an important distinction because *through our experiences of coping with everyday, "ordinary" challenges we learn resilience skills that we can put into place when faced with greater challenges or tragedy.*

> *Resilience is our response to challenge.*

And isn't this what we want for our children: the ability to face successfully all that life offers them, both the good and the bad?

Let's explore how.

Chapter Two

Teachable Moments: Turning Challenges into Opportunities

Teachable moments are everywhere. Let's take a look at one.

A little boy at a playground drops his toy; it lands in a spot where he can't reach it. He sits down and screams for his mother, who is on the other side of the playground, until she comes over to pick up the toy for him.

This is a perfect opportunity for the mom to teach her boy how to solve the problem in a more effective manner. Since her son is standing right next to an adult, she could tell her child to politely ask the grownup, "Could you please reach down and get my toy for me?"

But the opportunity is missed. Why? *Because in most parenting situations, grownups are reactive.* A child cries and the mom (or dad) reacts to his needs.

When we react, however, we sometimes miss great opportunities. Here's the lesson that little boy learned: *when I am having trouble, I can cry and my mom will come fix it for me.* Now, if the mom had been proactive, thinking ahead about opportunities to build resilience, she could have used this as a teachable moment—a moment to TEACH resilience.

This is true for every kind of challenge, although it is most important to start teaching resilience when children are still young.

Facing Life's Challenges

There are three basic types of challenges that characterize our experiences: developmental, conflict, and tragedy (potential and real). *Developmental challenges* are the natural challenges that people face as they grow and develop skills: running, biking, independence skills, etc. *Conflicts* are the social challenges presented as we interact with others. *Dangers* are challenges that place us in physical or emotional danger.

Thankfully, when children are young, the challenges that they likely will experience most often are developmental and conflict. This affords parents a great opportunity because these kinds of challenges give us manageable venues through which we can teach our children how to handle the greater difficulties that dangers and tragedies pose. Unfortunately, instead of taking advantage of these learning opportunities, parents often react.

Parenting is tough; our human nature makes it more difficult. We are emotional creatures, particularly when it comes to our children. Even if logically we know the right thing to do, we often aren't able to do it when emotions are involved because our emotions make us react. Let's take a look at each challenge and our natural reactions.

DEVELOPMENTAL

At each stage of life, there are challenges that we face that meet our developmental needs. These challenges represent opportunities to build *self-confidence* and *self-esteem*. As parents, it is important to recognize that all challenges present opportunities to lay the foundation for our children's future coping skills.

In order to be become independent beings, children need to face and handle common developmental challenges. They need to be able to walk, talk, and feed themselves. In our society, they need to be able to clear their plate, pick out their own clothes, order their own food at a restaurant, and make a living.

It's also true that facing developmental challenges can be painful. Our children can try to cross the monkey bars by themselves and end up falling. They can follow through with a commitment to be on a team and experience losing time and again as part of the team. So developmental challenges provide opportunities for growth . . . but in order to achieve growth, our children need to struggle first.

Now, when our children struggle, **our natural reaction is to protect** or help them. We love our children with all of our hearts, and, therefore we are "wired" to protect them! But our natural protective instinct developed at a time when parents needed to protect their children differently than they do today. It came about during a time when mankind's way of life required children to become more independent but placed them much more at risk for life-threatening challenges than occur today (for example, attacks by vicious predators). Parents back then needed to be on constant alert, and their brains were wired to offer the necessary protection to their kids.

So yes, it is natural to want to protect our children, and to hate to see them suffer. It can be very painful to sit and listen to our toddler cry out in the middle of the night, even if we know that he is fine and needs to learn the skill of putting himself back to sleep. That pain we experience comes from our love, as well as our natural instinct to protect.

In addition, the "self esteem movement" that emerged in the 1980's has given parents the idea that they need to provide their children with constant praise in order to raise their self-esteem. However, praise without struggle does not lead to feelings of satisfaction. According to Polly Young-Eisendrath, author of *The Self-Esteem Trap*, this movement has given rise to children that are obsessively self-focused, dissatisfied, and unready to take on adult responsibilities. Our instinct is to keep them from struggling, so we try to make they feel good through our praise. Unfortunately, this instinct is counter-productive.

We need to let our children fight their own battles and face their own failures—with our support and love, of course. To fight our counterproductive instinct, we need to be aware of it, and proactively avoid its dangers.

As author and columnist Lori Gottlieb writes in her article, "How to Land your Kid in Therapy," many children who experience normal frustrations are unable to handle them because their parents today shelter their children from experiencing even mild discomfort. Her viewpoint receives support from Wendy Mogel, author of

> *In order to fight our counter-productive instinct, we need to be aware of it, and proactively avoid its dangers.*

The Blessing of a Skinned Knee, who points to the fact that college deans are reporting that a growing number of college freshman are unable to handle even small problems. Undoubtedly this is how the term

"The Teacup Generation" came about in reference to the latest generation of children.

Kids need to face and handle challenges while their parents are there to guide them, as this helps prepare them for their future. If their parents do not allow them to have those experiences, and don't think about these experiences as teachable moments, they are denying them a great opportunity.

It may sound counterintuitive, but there is a huge benefit to allowing kids to struggle: it is through struggles and failures that children learn both confidence . . . and resilience.

CONFLICT

The second kind of challenge we all face is conflict. We are social creatures so we spend a lot of our time with other people. When one person wants one thing, but the other individual wants something else, there is a potential for conflict. Conflict develops when negotiation breaks down, and the natural **reaction to the conflict that ensues is anger.**

Here's the problem—when we are emotional, our brain's prefrontal cortex, a.k.a. its "command center," may get knocked out of commission:

When we get upset...a part of our brain called the amygdala takes over; this emotional center literally hijacks the prefrontal cortex, which governs our decisions. You have the classic fight-or-flight response, during which you can't learn, innovate or be flexible; your memory is hampered, and all you can feel is threat."

---

*U.S. News & World Report

When we are emotional, we do not think straight, and often, we do things that we regret later. (Interestingly, the same thing happens as we are faced with threats and other potentially risky situations.)

When our children are young, we can use the conflicts they experience *as opportunities to teach them how to override the amygdala (or emotional center) and get their command center back.* And interestingly enough, proactive parenting also provides us parents with strategies to get our own command centers back. (We'll show you how later in this book.)

DANGER (POTENTIAL AND REAL)

Ultimately, resilience helps us to handle danger, potential or real. As human beings, our **natural reaction to danger is fear or avoidance.** After all, as parents, don't our greatest fears for our kids lie in such potential dangers as: bullying, abuse, illegal use of drugs and alcohol, and so on? We know all about the prevalence of these dangers in our society and so do our children. However, as grownups we also are very aware that peer pressure is an incredibly strong force—*so strong that it can override our children's healthy understanding of, and avoidance or rejection of, such dangers.*

Because we are social creatures, acceptance and approval are extremely powerful forces for us. In the 1960's, researcher Henry Milgram conducted an experiment in which he measured the willingness of people to obey an authority figure who told them to do something that conflicted with their conscience. In the experiment, he asked participants to administer high voltage shocks to someone whom they believed to be a fellow participant. The results of the experiment were disturbing: 65 percent of the participants administered what they thought to be a full series of shocks *simply because the experimenter encouraged them to continue.* Why did they go along with inflicting such pain on another person? *Because humans have a particularly strong ability to justify their actions in order to seek approval.*

In many ways, we are wired for such justifications. Our brains work on heuristics, quick rules of thumb for taking actions. One of these rules is the acceptance heuristic. That is what tells us not to "rock-the-boat" if it might put us at risk socially. As parents, we hope that our children will be able to make smart decisions in which they do "what's right," but unfortunately, social science research shows us that most often, *even adults do not.*

So exactly what do we base our response to life's challenges, whether they be small or large, on?

How We Respond to Life's Challenges

Our response to any challenge, small or large, is based on our understanding of these four things:

1- SELF: what we think about who we are, what we stand for, and what we are capable of.

2- SITUATION: our ability to accurately assess the challenge before us.

3- SUPPORT: our knowledge of our support structures and how to access them.

4- STRATEGIES: our ability to access and use effective strategies to handle the challenge.

When we face any challenge, we draw on our understanding of these Four Ss.

For example, recently a group of elementary students we know hosted a pancake breakfast to raise money for charity. Everything was set to go: they had rented industrial griddles (placed in the hallway because the kitchen was so small) and at about 8:50 am, they started cranking out pancakes. The challenge? The griddles had tripped the fuse because the electrical system was not designed to handle such a power draw. In walked the first customers, with no pancakes and cold coffee.

The response drew from the Four Ss:

- SELF: The kids and parents needed to know that they could find alternate solutions—that they had the ability to draw on other plans.

- SITUATION: They needed to evaluate the situation and understand that they could find other solutions. One person immediately moved into the kitchen and started frying pans on the stove, another started microwaving coffee cups one at a time, a third started rounding up home griddles, and a forth went to find the head of school to locate the circuit breaker. In other words, they worked together to put a plan in place.

- SUPPORT: They knew how to draw upon several support structures: other community members with home griddles, the head of school, and the custodian (who happened to walk in minutes after the fuse had tripped).

- STRATEGIES: Both the kids and the adults used multiple strategies to address the challenge. They found ways to meet the immediate needs while coming up with a long-term solution to the problem (finding a few kitchen griddles and knowing where the fuse was located in case it tripped again). The pancake breakfast was a success. Why? Because they used the challenge as an opportunity to teach resilience.

Proactive parenting is being able to use the Four Ss as a rubric for everyday challenges to teach our children resilience. It involves *being able to understand our natural reactions, using certain tools to override those reactions, and using that challenge to teach resilience. When we can do this, we are proactive, not reactive.*

PART TWO

The Framework: The Four Ss for Challenges

→

Chapter Three

◆·◆·◆

Scaffolding: Parenting for Independence and Problem-Solving

The goal of parenting is to become an empty-nester who has kids who can take really good care of themselves. Now, *have you just balked at this statement?*

Even if you did, the truth is clear: *Your kids need to be able to think, behave, and make decisions that allow them to be independent and functional **without you.***

One day, all parents should hope to wave goodbye and wish their children well as they venture off into a new home and life for themselves. Kind of funny, isn't it? It sounds like our goal as parents is to, well, render ourselves useless! Well, not to be really useless, but at least in a position where our children *want us but don't need us because they can take care of themselves, emotionally and behaviorally.*

> Your kids need to be able to think, behave, and make decisions that allow them to be independent and functional without you.

Here is an e-mail that we received recently from a parent of four very independent teens:

Many teenagers break down because they haven't been taught independence skills. I have seen so many kids have a terrible time with the basics of laundry, cleaning and making a schedule. Practicality and common sense are just as important as book knowledge to be able to deal with the pressures of the world.

In her book *Don't Give Me That Attitude!*, child expert Dr. Michele Borba refers to this lack of responsibility as a part of the "Big Brat Factor." In her book, she offers some great suggestions about how to curb this trend. Time and again, we are hearing the same story from other educators: they are seeing *a steady decline in basic independence skills.* They are struck by how, across the board, today's generation of children seems less able to problem-solve.

Independence Breeds Competence

Independence breeds the feeling of competence. And when kids feel competent, they gain an improved sense of self. So kids need to have opportunities to do things themselves as early as possible.

> Independence breeds the feeling of competence.

We are not doing our children any favors by doing things for them. Yes, in many ways it is easier to do things yourself, because as a grownup with life experience, you're faster and more competent than they are at the task or experience at hand. However, it is better for children if *they learn to do things themselves.* This is how we prepare our children to be independent, capable creatures, and this is teaching them *resilience.*

In proactive parenting, your job is to <u>be a teacher</u>, not to be a more competent and successful person than your child.

Teaching What Needs to be Taught in Our New Technology Age

When we think about teaching, many of us picture the traditional teaching model of an adult standing in front of a classroom lecturing to students, with the students ultimately learning the material and spitting it back for the test. We call this teaching method the "etch-a-sketch" model of teaching, as the students cram all of the information into their heads to pass the test. But once they leave, they merely give their heads a little shake—and the information is all gone!

In their parenting, many adults mirror that traditional teaching style. Unfortunately, parental lectures have much the same effect—without the test.

Times have changed, and our teaching and parenting need to as well.

Remember how the adults all sounded in Charlie Brown? "Wah, Wah . . . Wah . . . Wah . . . ." Everything the adults said went in one ear (barely), then out the other.

The traditional teaching model was designed in a different time, when the goal of education was not to create strong, independent beings, but to spit out compliant beings who followed directions ably. Well, times have changed, and our teaching and parenting need to as well.

The traditional teaching model is outdated because in this day and age, we <u>need to raise kids who are able to think critically</u> <u>and make</u>

39

independent decisions. We want adults who can work cooperatively with one another in our global economy to design creative solutions to problems. In this new millennium of our exploding technology age (with its ever-growing worldwide web), it isn't as important to simply memorize and spit out information. It is more important than ever to be able to locate, assimilate, and evaluate information—and that is what we need to teach our children.

Teachers who are highly effective today encourage students to actively engage in their learning through the use of cooperative learning projects and hands-on activities. "Good" teachers don't spend a great deal of time lecturing; instead, they present questions and guide students on their own quests to find the answers. And through these methods, students are more likely to learn how to think, investigate, and communicate with others. Therefore, they are more likely to remember the information that is learned.

The great teacher has moved from "Sage on the Stage" to "Guide on the Side," and teaching has changed . . . from directing to scaffolding.

Scaffolding

A building is being constructed. When the building is being built, the workers set up a scaffold in order to support its safe construction. Gradually, though, as the construction is finished and the building is more secure, the scaffold is removed. In much the same way, the job of the teacher or parent—when teaching ANYTHING—is to provide *temporary* support while simultaneously teaching strategies for learning. So when a child is first learning a skill, the teacher or parent will provide lots of support, *but as the child learns, the teacher or parent gradually provides less and less until none is needed and the child is able to do the task independently.* Through the scaffolding process, parents and teachers give children greater and greater freedom and the latitude to be on their own as they learn the skills needed to function independently.

Probably the clearest example of providing scaffolding is shown through teaching someone how to ride a bike. First, the instructor gives a lot of support—holding the bike steady while running alongside it with hands on both bike and the child to help the child experience the feeling of riding along without training wheels. Gradually, though, the instructor removes some of that support—perhaps the hand from the front is slowly removed while the hand on back of the bike is still held on firmly. Next, though, he loosens his grip on the back. As the rider gains confidence, the instructor completely lets go, but stays close, ready to quickly grab onto and hold the bike and rider if necessary. Gradually, though, he moves further and further away until the rider finally goes off on his or her own.

Learning to ride a bike is a *process*. For some kids, it takes longer than others. Some kids take steps backward—maybe they take a fall and need to go back to having more support. Some kids hop on without any trouble at all and manage to maintain their balance all by themselves. When you are their teacher, it is your job to provide as much support as a child needs.

Scaffolding Paves the Way . . . for a Home Run

Okay, let's take a look at another concrete example: learning how to hit a baseball. When a child is first trying to hit the ball, the parent might purchase a t-ball set, which places a ball slightly bigger and softer than a baseball on a stand so the ball does not move. The parent will start showing the child how to hit by standing beside him and helping him hold and swing the bat. As the child tries to connect with the ball, the parent provides supportive comments even if the child is not connecting with the ball or is failing to stand properly. Gradually, the grownup will loosen his grip until the child is aiming and swinging on is own. Once the child becomes able to hit the ball from a tee, the parent can move on in the instruction process by trying to pitch a ball very slowly and directly at the child's bat. Eventually, the child is ready to hit a ball on his own, and there is no need for any more scaffolding.

Scaffolding is *teaching*. Not lecturing, not yelling, but *teaching*: supporting and providing structures that support learning. Make sense?

Okay, let's move on to a less concrete example. Most young kids need to develop organizational skills. They do not naturally keep their belongings organized, so most need a bit of help. So how can we "scaffold" organization skills?

First, we can provide physical structures, such as cubby spaces, toy bins, and shelves. Next, we need to teach our kids to use these structures. We scaffold first through a physical process: we literally show our kids how to put their things in the right place, and/or physically do it with them. Next, we provide them with support as they do it themselves: we provide verbal feedback on how to do it and assist only when needed. Eventually, we expect them to do it themselves. True, there will always be slips and times when they need reminders from us. This is all a part of scaffolding.

At schools, teachers scaffold in much the same way. When good teachers first give their young students long-term assignments, they often break them down into tasks, provide checklists, and give several interim deadlines. Many schools now even provide checklists and homework books that help students to complete the tasks that they are expected to do. Increasingly popular teaching tools are graphic organizers that scaffold students' ability to outline information or complete long writing assignments. People used to think using these supports was "cheating," but now we realize that they are simply good teaching constructs. They help show the way

Ultimately, scaffolding allows children to become more independent by providing as much support as necessary at the time and gradually removing that support as the children master the skill or task at hand.

so that kids learn to be more independent. Ultimately, scaffolding allows children to become more independent by providing as much support as necessary at the time and gradually removing that support as the children master the skill or task at hand.

Parenting for independence is all about providing the appropriate scaffold.

The bottom line: *If they can do it themselves, let them. If they can't, give them the support they need, gradually pulling back until they can do it on their own. Remember: that's the goal of parenting!*

———◆◆◆———

Chapter Four

The Resilient Mindset: Parenting for Effective Thinking and Communication Skills

Resilience is built on learning how to respond to the challenges that lie in front of us. One of our jobs as parents is to teach our kids the coping strategies they need to respond effectively. Dr. Robert Brooks and Sam Goldstein, authors of *The Power of Resilience,* talk about resilience as a mindset. Proactive parents need to scaffold a mindset in children about how they should think and communicate with others.

In a recent TEDx talk, Dr. Dan Siegel suggests that school curriculums should be focused on the more important 3 Rs: reflection, relationships and resilience. It is through our reflection and formation of relationships—our ability to think and communicate—that we are able to build a resilient mindset.

Therefore, proactive parents need to scaffold a mindset in children about how they should think and communicate with others. It's a two-part process.

1- HOW WE THINK

The first step to developing resilience lies in our thought processes. The experiences we have as children afford us with our first opportunities to think about the world. These thought patterns are learned and reinforced when we are children, and over time become very ingrained in our minds.

Each interaction that we have—from the time we are born through adulthood—contributes to our thought patterns, *and the responses that we get from our own experiences and others pattern our future behavior.*

Take, as an example, a newborn baby. As that baby goes out with his mother, he has experiences. Maybe he is in the grocery store and a stranger looks down and smiles at him. If the newborn smiles back, the stranger probably continues to shower attention on him. If, however, the baby does not respond, the stranger is likely to move on quickly. The smile that the child gives reinforces the interaction, and, therefore, those babies who smile easily are more likely to have their interactions reinforced. The baby who smiles and has their interaction reinforced then becomes more likely to smile again in the future, creating a pattern of behavior.

> Parents can help children to interpret the interactions that they have and teach them ways to foster more positive interactions.

Parents have the opportunity to guide children in their interactions and their thoughts. We can help them to interpret the interactions that they have and teach them ways to foster more positive interactions. For example, when a child does have a negative interaction, we can talk through how they might change their behavior to get a more positive interaction the next time.

The thoughts we have are typically based in language. *As we think, we are, in effect, talking to ourselves.* Therefore, parents can guide their children's thinking by providing them language to interpret these situations. Because our thoughts are based in language, we actively promote thinking through our attempts at verbal communication.

2- HOW WE COMMUNICATE

"Use your words!" This parental phrase is commonly expressed, but so often what results is disappointing: our children do not know what words to use or how to use them—that is, unless we actively teach them.

Why don't parents realize this? We read to a child, send them to school, and teach them the alphabet because we do not expect them to learn to read on their own. What we are doing here is teaching them *strategies.* Most parents take for granted that their kids will learn to communicate effectively on their own or through schooling, but the reality is, good communication doesn't come naturally: it needs to be taught. Our kids need strategies.

What are the results of poor communication? Think about all the unhealthy marriages out there: when there is bad communication between two spouses, it leads to arguments and control battles. The same results hold true for child-child and parent-child interactions.

We often can't always give our children the best approach to, and skills for, what they need because *many of us as adults do not have the best communication skills ourselves!* Fortunately, adults as well as children *can learn this skill.* Helping professionals and marriage counselors have created a business out of helping grownups and children alike communicate effectively . . . simply because effective communication can be learned.

The Importance of Effective Communication Skills

Being able to communicate effectively is a valuable skill for many reasons. First, it enables us to **convey our needs**. How often do we adults have problems communicating our own needs? Are we really always able to tell our husband that we're tired from juggling too many balls? Are we ever able to suggest to our wife that we need some private time for ourselves? Not all of the time, right? Now let's think about our children. *Most conflict arises because kids do not know how to communicate what they want in an appropriate and effective way.* Instead of asking for a toy, they grab. Instead of asking to be included in the group, they tease. Instead of telling someone that they have a crush on that they want to go out on a date, they sext the person they like. *When we cannot convey our needs, we feel helpless . . . and often get ourselves into trouble.*

Effective communication allows kids to:

1- Convey their needs

2- Prevent and handle conflict

3- Stay safe

Second, being able to communicate effectively allows us to **prevent and handle conflict**. Using words effectively to avoid conflict or to negotiate a conflict is extremely powerful. Too often, kids immediately turn to an adult to negotiate that conflict for them—and too often, today's adult does just that. *When adults resolve conflict for their children* rather than teaching them how to do it themselves, it disempowers children and fosters a dependency on adults to manage their disagreements and conflicts for them.

Third, effective communication can provide our children with the **skills that they need to stay safe.** *The sense of power that kids develop from negotiating conflicts successfully converts into the power that they have to avoid or negotiate danger.* You see, they have learned that they can stand up for themselves. They have learned that they can effect change. They have learned not to become silent victims.

When adults say, "Use your words," they really expect children to know how to use them. But unless they have been given those words and been given ample opportunity and strategies to practice those words, they honestly do not know how.

The Framework for Proactive Parenting

In order to teach our kids resilience, we need to be able to teach them how to handle challenges. As we stated in Chapter Two, our response to any challenge is guided by our understanding of four things: *self, situation, support, and strategies.*

Therefore, to handle challenges, our young people need to learn to **think** and **communicate** effectively. They need to be able to *think* realistically about **themselves** and the **situations** that they face, and they need to be able to *communicate* effectively in order to access their **support** systems and use effective **strategies**.

> *We want to teach our children to think clearly to evaluate self and situation, and have the communication skills to access important support systems and strategies.*

As parents, we want to teach our children to think clearly to evaluate **self and situation,** and have the communication skills to access **important support systems and strategies.** That, in a nutshell, is our framework for proactive parenting.

Okay, let's take a little breather here and review:

- Resilience is our response to challenge.

- We can use everyday challenges to teach resilience.

- Our resilience is determined by our understanding of the Four Ss.

- We can scaffold our children's understanding of the Four Ss through everyday challenges.

Chapter Five

————◆◆◆————

The Four Ss:
When Our Kids Face
Everyday Challenges

Remember, when any one of us faces a challenge, big or small, our reaction is guided by our understanding of the Four Ss: self, situation, support, and strategies. These four concepts make up the foundation to handle any challenge.

Let's return to the challenge that the little boy faced in Chapter Two: he dropped his toy and could not reach it. How he responds to this is guided by his developmental understanding of:

> *The Four Ss make up the foundation to handle any challenge.*

1- SELF: What does he think about himself and his abilities? Does he first evaluate whether or not he can figure out how to get the toy on his own? Is he confident enough to give it a try?

2- SITUATION: How does he evaluate the situation? Is it just a small problem or is it a huge issue? Is it something that can be handled and the end goal reached, or is it hopeless?

3- SUPPORT: Does he have a support system that he can draw upon to help him through the situation? If so, does he know how to access that support system? Does he have other supports in place in case the first one is not available?

4- STRATEGIES: Does he have specific strategies to meet his needs? Can he come up with alternate strategies?

Ideally, to feel and show resilience, that little boy will have enough confidence in himself to try to reach the toy and possibly look for something to help him resolve the situation—perhaps a stick that he can use to try and draw the toy over to him. If these attempts are not successful, can he rely on another strategy? Can he ask his mom for help, or if he realizes she is not available, look to others for assistance and support? If he could evaluate who would be best to ask for help, he could use the strategies he knows to politely ask for help from a grown-up nearby.

In older children, familiarity and comfort with the Four Ss translates to different, more dangerous types of challenges. A junior in high school has been at a party and realizes that his ride home is a senior who smells of alcohol. The Four Ss that come into play here are the same:

1- SELF: What does he think about himself and his abilities? Does this junior evaluate whether he can figure out an effective way to get out of the situation on his own? Does he say something to the senior? Is he confident enough in his abilities to find a different way home? Does he put his safety on the line and take the chance because he is afraid of upsetting the senior?

2- SITUATION: How does he evaluate the situation? Does he view it as a "small" problem or a huge issue because he may be getting into a car with someone his own age that smells of alcohol? Is this a situation that he can handle, or is it a huge social risk to stay out of the car?

3- SUPPORT: Does he have a support system that he can draw upon to help him through the situation? Does he know how to access that support system? Does he know how to reach his parent, or find a friend? Does he have other systems in case the first is not available? Can he call a neighbor to come get him? Can he ask to sleep over at the house of the host of the party and avoid having to face the drunken-driving issue?

4- STRATEGIES: What specific strategies does he have to get his needs met? Can he suggest that he be the driver if his drunken friend starts pressuring him to get into the car? Does he have alternative strategies that he can draw from, i.e., texting an adult to show up and help him?

Let's digress for a moment. We all know the phrase, "Just Say 'No.'" But many of us have come to realize that "Just say 'no'" may not always be the right strategy. Many of us don't follow it in the first place, because of what is called the "acceptance heuristic" (page 31), which reflects "our strong tendency to make choices that will get us noticed—and more importantly approved—by others."* Scientists are finding that this tendency to try to be noticed by others is hard-wired—a part of the neurological make-up of our brains.

---

*U.S. News & World Report

The implication is that in order to make resilient choices, *we sometimes need to defy a strong natural tendency (see page 31 as a reminder)*. In order to do this, we need to be prepared.

What is the takeaway as parents from our teen in this example? We want him to have the ability to analyze challenging situations, recognize appropriate actions, and have the strategies to follow through on those actions. We want him to realize that getting in the car with a drunk driver is not safe and know how to get out of the situation by making different choices. We hope that he knows of several alternative strategies, from handling it himself ("Dude, can I drive your car? If we got pulled over, you're never gonna get to play in the game on Friday!") to drawing upon his support systems for help (texting another friend, parent, or neighbor to show up unexpectedly).

Filling Your Child's Tool Box

The more tools that a child has in their own "tool kit" of the Four Ss, the more resilient they become. At **www.toolkitsforkids.com**, there are a variety of tool kits designed to teach elementary and middle/high school students specific emotional life skills. These life skills will help kids cope with the many stressors and emotional triggers they face in everyday life by helping them assess and build their confidence, deal with worry and anxiety, and strengthen resilience. Here are a few examples of some of the activities:

◆ LOOKING CONFIDENT *(see figure 1)*
When children are faced with difficulties such as teasing or bullying, their confidence may be damaged. Confident kids have an easier time managing through bullying challenges because they are less likely to be shaken when other kids test out bullying behaviors on

Figure 1

SAMPLE TOOL from the Charge Up Your Confidence® Tool Kit for Kids
(Elementary School Edition)
www.toolkitsforkids.com

COURTESY OF TOOL KITS FOR KIDS LLC

them. This activity teaches kids to look and behave in confident ways even if they don't feel confident. They learn to look people in the eye when speaking, stand up straight, speak loudly enough and slowly enough to be heard, and keep a happy face without looking worried or scared. Practicing these skills helps kids develop confidence because looking confident projects an image that shows other kids they are not easily shaken, and this increases their social capital.

◆ IT'S NOT A DIFFICULT FOREVER

What if your middle school child loses an important friendship due to a move, change in schools or a fight they had? How can we help them deal with this and feel stronger? Remember that our child's brain may be very emotional and their perspective of loss will probably not be developed for many years. This activity helps teens develop accurate thinking by teaching a long-term perspective on time. The following thoughts can be rehearsed over and over again to help their brain develop the language needed to help them gain this perspective and help them get through today:

- This is a difficult time. It's not a difficult forever.
- I may feel bad now, but I may feel better later.
- My life may not be OK now, but in time, I can find a new way to be OK.

The accurate thoughts about time help kids adjust their thinking to the troubles they have right now and introduce the possibility of feeling better, later.

These tool kits offer strategies for kids that help them think about the Four Ss. Now, let's take a look at each of the Four Ss individually. The first two Ss, self and situation, inform the way that we *evaluate the challenge*. The second two Ss, support and strategies, *inform the way we act.*

Evaluate the Challenge: Relying on **Self**

By *self*, we mean a person's understanding of his or her own abilities. It is *our assessment of our own ability to face challenges.* When we are faced with challenges or dangerous situations, our understanding of our "self" helps determine how we respond to that situation. If we have a strong sense of self:

- we are likely to view challenges positively;
- we are able to recover quickly from setbacks;
- we focus on our positive characteristics and abilities when handling a situation; and

- we have a *realistic understanding or perception* of our strengths, weakness, values, and goals.

Now, if we have a weak sense of self:

- we are likely to view challenges as roadblocks;
- we focus on and emphasize our failings; and
- we are quick to lose confidence in our abilities.

When faced with a dilemma, someone with strong sense of self is more likely to make a choice that benefits him or her in the long run.

Let's think back to Chris Waddell, the collegiate skier who was paralyzed. A lifelong athlete, he was faced with the knowledge after his accident that he would not be able to walk again. Here's the first of our Four Ss in action: Self. Instead of focusing on walking again (he was realistic about his self and his abilities, and he knew his physical self was altered in an unchangeable way), he turned his attention to the things he hoped he could still do. One of his first questions (which came about while he was still in the hospital) turned out to be: "When can I ski again?" (Chris knew that technology existed to help other paralyzed skiers continue skiing.) His focus on what his "self" could still do in his new current reality helped him see a future path. This is a seed for successful resilience.

> As parents, we need to help our children to have an accurate and realistic understanding of self.

As parents, we need to help our children to have an *accurate* and *realistic* understanding of self—both the "good" parts and the "bad" parts. In her book, *The Self-Esteem Trap*, Polly Young-Eisendrath, Ph.D., points to a new trend of unhappiness found in young adults.

~~These young adults have difficulty living up to their expectations given their belief that they should be extraordinary. Raised during the self-esteem movement, they have always been told that they are "special." In childhood, mediocre effort was always met with overwhelming praise, but now, as they face adulthood, they find that expectations are much higher. These mismatched expectations of self and reality create confusion for them and they find themselves consistently disappointed.~~

Self-esteem needs to be built on a realistic understanding of one's abilities. We do not help our children build a realistic sense of self if we exaggerate their abilities or try to hide their struggles. Instead, parents can actively guide their children to a better understanding of themselves.

BRANDING

In the business world, large corporations often hire a branding expert to come in and lead them through activities designed to solidify their corporate identity. Similarly, parents can guide their children to an understanding of their unique "brand." This includes a discussion of their strengths, weaknesses, and values through a self-reflective process.

At **www.urresilient.com**, a branding tool can be found that guides users through a variety of activities designed to help them actively think about who they are and what their values are—their personal brand. This tool, which can be used in schools and other institutions, is called URBrand™. By completing the activities thoughtfully, kids gain a better understanding of themselves and their goals. Once they complete the activities, they can print out and share a trifold that represents that brand *(See figure 2)*.

Here is an example of one of the activities, which can be done at home:

Figure 2

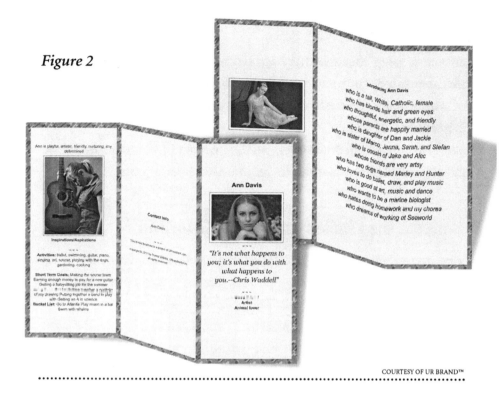

This activity, which we call "If You Were . . . ," helps children further their understanding of their unique strengths and weaknesses. When the family is together (perhaps seated around the lunch or dinner table), each person gets a chance to supply the category for the question, 'If you were . . . [subject area], what would you be?" Categories include things like a car, a food, a piece of furniture, a television show, or an animal. Each member of the family then answers the question. Once someone says what she would be, she must then supply why she gave that answer. In response, other members of the family (or friends, etc.) may offer other suggestions.

The most important part comes from the "why," which the respondent must supply with his or her answer. He or she must name the qualities that support his or her answer. Someone might choose a "Jeep" because they are rugged and easy-going. A family member might counter that response and say, "I think you are more of a mini-van because family is so important to you and a mini-van is a family car."

There are no right answers, and the primary idea is to get everyone talking about personal qualities in a non-threatening way.

Evaluate the Challenge: Rely on **Situation**

The second foundation for resilience is *situation: our ability to accurately assess the situation when a challenge takes place, and our ability to put the challenge into perspective.*

In many ways, our assessment of the situation has to do with our emotional reaction to the situation at hand: *Do we get overwhelmed or panic? Do we think clearly and do what needs to be done?* Everyone faces little and big challenges all the time. *How can we help our children recognize the difference and keep it in perspective?* How we assess the challenge largely determines how we react and feel. Here's an example of great perspective that demonstrates a resilient mindset:

> **Situation:** our ability to accurately assess the situation within which a challenge takes place, and our ability to put the challenge into perspective.

Ann's seventeen-year-old son was in the hospital. His lung had collapsed for the second time, and he had received an operation to fix it. A friend asked Ann how she was holding up. She replied, "You know, it was really tough at first, but once the operation was done and we knew he was going to be okay, I realized that I had such a great opportunity to spend quality time with my son. I am not sure if I will ever get that chance again [because he's growing up so fast], so I really kind of enjoyed spending the time with him in the hospital. I got to be a mom again." Now, *that* is *perspective*. How many people would have been able to face that challenge and recognize the gift it offered?

For others, a slight bump-in-the-road can be tragic. Many school administrators can relay stories of parents fiercely fighting to get grades changed or challenging the fact that their child did not make a school team, fearing that if they do not fix the situation their child will never be accepted into college. These moments are difficult but not tragic, and when parents overdramatize them, kids learn to do the same.

The ability to put challenges of all kinds into perspective is a gift that we want to instill in our children, and it is a significant part of resilience. For some kids, that perspective seems to come naturally. For others, it takes a lot more work but can be learned with practice.

Are we allowing our children to have this opportunity to learn perspective from handling little challenges? Maybe not. In a recent *New York Times* article, researchers question the trend of creating "safety-first" playgrounds (no jungle-gyms/ cushioned landings throughout). They point out the risk

> *The ability to put challenges of all kinds into perspective is a gift that we want to instill in our children, and it is a significant part of resilience.*

this trend poses for stunting children's emotional development, leaving "... children with anxieties and fears that are ultimately worse than a broken bone." In other words, if our children do not receive the opportunity to learn from small falls, they do not gain the perspective needed to evaluate a situation accurately. In the future, they won't be able to assess if a six-foot-jump off a tree or wall is manageable or catastrophic, for example.

Informs How We Act: Using **Supports**

Support, the third foundation for resilience, is *our ability to successfully utilize others for support and know we are not alone.* Support means that we know how to successfully reach out to others in difficult times. To do this, we need to identify those who can be of assistance and know how to garner their support. Support speaks to our ability to know when we need to reach out to someone, whom we need to reach out to, and how to effectively reach out to him.

> **Support** *speaks to our ability to know when we need to reach out to someone, whom we need to reach out to, and how to effectively reach out to him.*

This sounds like such an easy task, but in reality it is not. Think back to the little boy on the playground that screamed for his mom: he didn't understand that there were support systems besides his mom around him. Even if children are able to access one support system, it may not be enough. In a bullying situation, many kids are afraid to reach out to possible supports because they feel helpless, ashamed, and embarrassed. Or, they may reach out to a peer or another classmate who is unable to help and assume that others such as teachers, adults, family members, and administrators in a school will not be there to help even if in reality they may be effective support systems.

Helping children and teens find support in someone is a critical skill. We never want our kids to feel so alone that they feel helpless and give up trying to find a way out of a painful situation because they have no access to support. In extreme situations, kids may try to get support, but sometimes give up when they feel they haven't succeeded. Phoebe Prince was a Massachusetts teen who committed suicide after being bullied. She had reported the bullying to her teachers, but claimed that they did not respond, and ultimately she felt helpless.

It is difficult to know today if things may have changed had Phoebe felt safe to reach out to others again and again before her isolation became so extreme. As parents, we want our children to continue trying to find someone who can help until they encounter one who can offer the effective support, empathy, and understanding required to continue to fight through the pain.

The lesson from Phoebe's situation is that we need to help our kids find support by teaching them perseverance, persistence, and resilience. We can teach them to keep trying when they face a challenge. We can brainstorm with our child a list of people to build a network of support in their mind to rely on when they need more help. We can talk them through the small challenges, making suggestions of who to turn to in particular situations. We can talk about multiple scenarios, giving them opportunities to problem-solve and recognize a wider web of support.

How your child learns to access that network leads us to the next S: *Strategies*.

Informs the Way We Act: Using Our **Strategies**

The final foundation of resilience is being able to utilize specific strategies to meet the challenge at hand. *Strategies* are *the specific actions we take to handle the challenge.* We have to draw on our knowledge base to find a strategy to help meet a challenge, and if we discover that this particular strategic option doesn't work, we move on to alternative strategies to meet the goal.

> **Strategies** are the specific actions we take to handle the challenge.

This is how we build *tenacity—the ability to think creatively and keep going when faced with frustration*. As children build experience through brainstorming and problem-solving to meet early challenges in their lives, they build an arsenal of strategies, as well as gaining confidence. As parents, we teach them tenacity by reinforcing their practice of strategies with us early in their lives, and giving them latitude to do it on their own as they get older. (Letting go of the scaffold as they become more competent). Most of the time, strategies involve *knowing what language to use for the particular situation.* Here are some examples:

☺ *Preschool-age child:* A three-year-old boy comes into a room where other children are already playing. He spies a big toy truck that he wants to play with, but someone else is playing with it already. The three-year-old runs over to grab the toy away from the other child so he can play with it. The child accomplishes his mission, but we can teach our preschooler *a diplomatic and cooperative strategy that will fare better as he gets older.* We can teach him to walk over and say, "Can I have a turn with the truck when you are done (or: . . . after you dump the load it's carrying)?"

✎ *Elementary-school-age child:* When a seven-year-old girl goes to the park, she spies a group of girls playing together. The girl doesn't have a friend with her, and she would love to play with some girls her own age. As parents, we can teach her that one way to be invited to join the group is to approach the group and ask, "Hey, what are you guys playing? Can I join in?"

Teenager: A fifteen-year-old is caught smoking pot. He is admonished and punished, but we discover a text message on his phone the following week from someone who asked, "if he needed some for the holiday." The teenager's response was, "I don't know." When asked "What do you mean, 'you don't know?'" he responds in an anguished tone, "What else am I supposed to say? I have to seem cool to my friends—I'm just a freshman at this school, and I don't want them thinking I'm a nerd." Parents can help him with a script to take some pressure off the social heat he feels, by suggesting, "Tell him you got snagged by your parents and they came down really hard on you. They said if you are caught smoking again, you'll have to drop out of the lacrosse/soccer/baseball/swimming team, so thanks, but you just can't buy anything now." This script helped give this teen a "way out" that didn't cost him "social capital."

The Tool to Use in Moments of Challenge . . .

In moments of challenge, the Four Ss provide a framework for building resilience. They are a rubric for parents to consider as they help their children resolve the challenge and prepare to face other challenges. In the midst of emotion, the Four Ss provide a concrete and objective way of thinking about challenge.

Remember, through role-modeling, we are building the foundation for how our children will handle greater challenges in the future. If our children learn how to think positively about self and situation, and know how to communicate effectively to access support and strategies, they become more resilient . . . and prepared to handle challenges in the future.

How do we actually do this and give our children the tools they need? During moments of challenge when emotion takes over and thinking skills seem lost, can we provide our children with the ability to think and communicate effectively? How do we actually scaffold the Four Ss? The answer lies in . . . scripting.

Scripting is the tool that parents can use to scaffold thinking and communication about the Four Ss, and, therefore, build resilience. Scripting is a tool that works because it is based on an understanding of why and how our brain develops.

However, before we explain scripting, let us take a moment to illustrate the pattern of brain development our children have. Just as a mechanic needs to have a basic idea of how a car works before he sets about fixing it, we as parents need to have an understanding of how the brain develops before we set out to shape our children's brains.

◆◆◆

PART THREE

The Tool: Scripting for Success

→

Chapter Six

Developing Brains: Forging Paths in a Jungle

In the last ten years, there has been a significant change in our understanding of the brain—particularly that of the developing brain. Previously, scientists believed that the brain was pretty much fully developed by around age twelve. Now, we understand that it is not fully developed until the early twenties. The brain reaches 95 percent of its adult size by the age of six years, but after that time it still undergoes significant changes. The beauty of the brain during this period is its *plasticity,* or its *ability to change.* The best news? *As parents, we can have great impact on that development.*

It's a Jungle in There!

Picture the brain as a very large jungle. When a baby is born, that jungle is so overgrown that it is virtually impossible to get through. The jungle is filled with neurons (cells that transmit nerve impulses), but they are not particularly organized and effective; they operate more like tangled, going-nowhere vines. As the child learns, it signals the beginning of thinking, and this begins to clear pathways through that jungle. These pathways that are being cleared are really synapses letting the neurons send signals to the cells. As the synaptic pathways get clearer, it becomes easier to send those signals. The more those pathways are taken, the clearer they become. As children have different experiences and begin to learn new things, it clears those synaptic pathways.

As parents, we are in the position of being able to choose which pathways to clear in our children's brains. What we mean by this is that as parents, we make choices to expose our children to particular experiences (i.e., music lessons, reading, engaging in certain sports, playing on playgrounds, or video gaming), and it is those experiences that shape which pathways are cleared through our children's brains. *Those experiences that challenge the brain lay down pathways that children can draw upon later in their lives. Those pathways that are cleared and continually used form our children's thinking.*

> *As parents, we are in the position of being able to choose which pathways to clear in our children's brains.*

Now, if a section of the "jungle" is not used, that section eventually disappears. In other words, when it comes to brain development, it is literally "use it or lose it." *If we do not actively use certain parts of the brain, they get pruned away and lost.* This is why a young child can learn a foreign language without an accent, but when she tries to learn languages later in life, she cannot quite get the accent right. The brain pathways for some of the particular sounds are gone. They were pruned away because they were not being used.

That is also why as we age we try to keep our brain pathways stimulated, so we don't lose them.

How Parents Shape Their Children's Brains

As parents, our job is to help shape which brain pathways are cleared and which are to be pruned away. The choices that we make can help to shape our children's brains. Synaptic pathways that are reinforced are continually fine-tuned; the ones that are unused are discarded because they aren't needed. Over time, with continued use, the pathways that are cleared form people's thinking:

> As a child learns to associate symbols in the environment, certain pathways within the brain are reinforced . . . . As a child begins to associate images with words, these electrochemical messages become routine . . . . The more often the pathway is used, the more sensitive the pathway becomes and the more developed that pathway becomes in the individual brain. As these pathways develop, the collective group of used pathways becomes the map of how an individual thinks, reasons and remembers. Neurons which are not stimulated in these pathways tend to wither away and become unusable.*

The important point here is that *we can help choose those pathways that are reinforced and those that are not.* We make choices about what experiences our children have, and this helps to determine their brain development.

---

*Dr. Gene Van Tassell, brains.org

Words We Say Make All the Difference

Because we all think in language, we can use language as a tool to help reinforce specific pathways, particularly in our children's early years. For example, as we narrate the world for our children and feed them language, we create pathways. As our children are approaching a playground, we might say, "Let's head over to the sand area. I see a few kids playing with trucks and I know that you like to play trucks. Can you walk over to the boy in the red shirt and say "Hi, I'm Sam. Can I play with you?" As we repeat this process, the synaptic pathways become more refined and cleared, shaping thoughts and behaviors. Research reveals that children who grow up in language-rich environment prosper. This is because, especially in those first six years, language is a critical part of developing synaptic pathways.

In the first six years, language is a critical part of developing the brain's synaptic pathways.

During a person's first eleven years, there is a consistent thickening of the gray matter, which is the thinking part of the brain. Much like a tree grows branches, the gray matter thickens as new pathways and experiences are added. The development of this gray matter peaks at around age eleven in girls and age twelve in boys—roughly the same time as the onset of puberty.

However, these pathways that are created in the first eleven years are only a blueprint for the brain that will evolve. Remember that we said that the beauty of the brain in its early years is the plasticity? The pathways that we help to clear during the early years are *rough*—they are like dirt pathways, rather than paved, and they are still vulnerable and open to change. At about twelve years of age though, the brain hits a critical point: it begins to construct the more permanent brain.

The Teenage Years: Heavy-Construction-Zone Time!

At about age twelve, the brain enters a heavy construction zone. From this time until the early twenties (when the brain is considered the "adult brain"), there are two main processes: 1) the pruning away of those synaptic pathways that have not been utilized; and 2) the solidifying or paving of those that have been used. Picture it this way: it is as if the synaptic pathways are moving from a temporary rental brain into a permanent brain.

Now, when we move to a new home, what do we typically do? First, we *purge*—getting rid of those things that we haven't used in a while. Well, the brain does the same thing. During the teenage years, there is a period of significant synaptic pruning—those synapses that have not been used get

From age 12 to the early 20's the brain:

1- *gets rid of unused pathways*

2- *solidify those pathways that were used*

pruned away and disappear. Scientists refer to this as the "use it or lose it" principle. Those synaptic pathways that are used survive and flourish. Those that are not are lost to us. *The parenting decisions we make help to decide which of those pathways remain in the brains of our children.*

Second, we try to make the new place we move to a bit nicer—more organized and efficient than our old home. The brain does the same thing. Those pathways that have been used get covered (or paved!) in order to make the sending of messages faster and more efficient, and the organizational structures become more sophisticated.

Interestingly, "brain construction" actually starts at the back of the brain when we are children, moving gradually to the front of the brain during the late teen and early adult years. The last zone to be constructed is the *prefrontal cortex*, the part of the brain responsible for judgment, planning, and impulse control.

Most of parental frustration with teenagers happens because the arrival of their judgment and control comes so late! You see, during the brain's construction, a teenager is particularly vulnerable to two cravings: *risk* and *social acceptance*. Without the advantage of having the prefrontal cortex established, a teenager is more prone to taking risks and experiencing great danger. This vulnerability to risk and social acceptance is evolutionary. Without it, teens might never have the drive to leave the safety and security of "the nest." *They need that drive in order to take the risk to become independent.*

Teenagers at Risk

Why then, we might ask, is the prefrontal cortex the last part of the brain to be constructed? The theory is that it is because of plasticity. Remember, all of our brain's efficiency and organization comes with a price: the brain becomes less flexible. Scientists believe that *the prefrontal cortex develops last in order to take advantage of that time period for great learning.*

Adolescence is a critical time period in the brain's development.

The period from puberty to adulthood is a time of great potential—and the critical time in which brain sculpting takes place. The prefrontal cortex has the advantage of plasticity during the majority of this time.

It is natural and beneficial for teens to take risks. Thus, *they need challenge in order to strengthen their synaptic pathways and prepare themselves to handle adult life.* As parents, we need to help our teens to take risks and handle challenges in a way that builds their resilience and keeps them from danger.

The simple reality is, adolescence is a critical time period in the brain's development. And the three main reasons for this are:

1- The pathways paved during this time become the more permanent structures of the adult brain. This may be our last opportunity as parents to pave those pathways in our children!

2- The brain becomes less flexible after adolescence.

3- This development is all taking place at a time when there is a need/drive for social acceptance and risk-taking.

Taking it a step further: since teenagers are more prone to taking risks, what can we do as parents to proactively protect them during this particular time period when they are especially vulnerable to dangerous situations? How do we prepare them to escape dangerous situations automatically—almost without having to think about it—and also work to develop the synaptic pathways that strengthen children's understanding of the Four Ss?

We use the tool of scripting—implementing its usage as early as possible in our children's lives.

———◆◆◆———

Chapter Seven

◆◆◆

Scripting:
Its Power and Process

In a perfect world, we would like to think of our children saying exactly what we want them to say and acting how we want them to act—but does that happen in reality? Much of the time, no. The power of scripting comes from the fact that, if our kids knew what to say and do, they would probably do it (most of the time). So, if we tell them exactly what to say or do, they often respond in the way that we like. _Scripting is the process of providing the exact language_

> *Scripting is the process of providing the exact language we want and having someone repeat it back.*

we want and having someone repeat it back. There's a much greater chance we'll get what we want if we script.

The _goal of scripting_ in this book is to provide kids with strategies to handle everyday challenges. The job of the adult is _to scaffold_: provide just enough support to teach the child a pathway they can begin to remember on their own with practice. Each time the child hears and repeats appropriate language, she is practicing and clearing that pathway in the brain. Just like the musician practices a musical piece, the child is practicing language. Scripting is a wonderful way to scaffold a child's learning because the job of the adult is to provide as much of the language as necessary and to gradually provide less and less so that the child becomes independent. As adults scaffold their children's language development through scripting, they are helping them create the neural pathways in their brains and provide them with the executive functions to manage these pathways effectively.

What is interesting to note is that the types of challenges children face do not change that much through the years. Therefore, *an early investment in scripting pays off because kids can apply the knowledge throughout their lives.*

The earlier you script with your children, the better. But it is never too late to start.

The Process

Okay...here we go: the basic two-step process of scripting:

STEP 1- CREATE THE SCRIPT.
As we said before, a critical step in scripting is to 'feed' the needed language to your child. In order to do this, you must *create the script for the given social situation.* To create the script, you need to consider the language *that the child needs.*

For many adults, this is the most difficult part because it requires a change in perspective. Adults are used to intervening and telling children what to do; they often have more difficulty thinking of the language that the child should use. You need to be sure to use *age-appropriate language*, not adult language. Remember, the goal is for your children to learn resilience—to be able to handle the challenge themselves or to access support systems appropri-ately—therefore, *they need to have the strategies that they would use, not you, so they can apply them in situations when an adult is not there.*

> The basic two-step process of scripting:
>
> **1-** Create the script.
> **2-** Repeat the phrase.

Here are a few examples of scripts that involve "kid language," which teach children to be polite and use their manners when they request something:

> "Mom, can I please have some more milk?"
> "Dad, would you please help me pour this juice?"
> "Sam, can I please have a turn with that?"
> "Mom, can I use the car to go to the mall with Tracey, please?"

Those are exact phrases that we want them to say, so we feed them those phrases, and then move to step two.

STEP 2- REPEAT THE ENTIRE PHRASE EXACTLY.

The second step to scripting is to make sure that the children repeat the exact phrase, in its entirety. Because the goal is to form a neural pathway, it is extremely important that when they repeat the language, they are repeating *the entire* phrase.

Imagine that your child wants a cookie. Here is the typical scenario:

> *Child:* Mom, can I have a cookie?
> *Mom:* What do you say?
> *Child:* Please.

What is the pathway that has been cleared here? It is only this: "Mom, can I have a cookie?" If your child does not repeat the whole phrase when you prompt them—"May I have a cookie, please?"—it does not clear the complete pathway and your chances of getting the "please" to become part of the phrase in your child's mind are slim to none.

One thing to note: research has shown that children are able to transfer the pathway established here to other requests, such as asking for a car or a cake. For some reason, they can replace the word "cookie" without changing the pathway—establishing the path to ask an adult for something— but "please" must consistently be made a part of it or it will get lost. So there it is: **the golden rule for raising a polite kid:** *have them say the whole phrase—don't let them separate out the "please!"*

Those are the two parts of the scripting process: *create the script* and *repeat the entire phrase exactly*. Those two little steps are so basic, but when used consistently, so powerful. You will be amazed at how they can be applied in almost any situation.

Before we move ahead to demonstrate how to use the power of scripting, we want to introduce a specific type of script, the trigger-script. Why? Because before we can script effectively, we need to deal with the two things that will obstruct our efforts, emotion and control.

We started the book with a story about Eric and his family, who were in crisis. Eric ran away in the heat of the moment—he was angry, full of raw emotional energy, and out of control. But then there are simply the control battles that rage on, too:

> ***Adult:*** Sam, just let me put this on; we need to get Jake and Lisa to school.

Sam: No, green one.

Adult: I don't know where your green one is; just put on this one.

Sam: No!

Adult: Sam, I said it is time to go. Just let me put this one on.

Sam: Noooooooo!!!!

Battles for control: these moments send parents' blood pressure soaring! At times like these, we are usually at our wits' end and running late, and now we need to deal with a *battle?* What should we do? Force them to do what we say? Or give in?

In our children's elementary years, we battle over cleaning rooms and finishing homework. In the middle school years, the battles tend to be about what they are wearing and how much time they are texting. In high school, we often battle about getting home late and use of the car.

> *Unfortunately, if parenting becomes about controlling our children, we have lost the battle.* **It doesn't work.**

So what do control battles have to do with resilience? Everything. These are the moments that test us, but it is also in these moments that kids learn the most about the foundations of resilience. So many parents spend their time in control battles with their kids. *Unfortunately, if parenting is about controlling our children, we have lost the battle. It doesn't work.* Just ask any parent who falls into the power battles: they feel exhausted and frustrated.

Proactive parenting is about using scripting to teach the Four Ss, but sometimes, that can't be done right away, particularly when we are dealing with emotion and control.

Emotion & Control

Through research findings on the brain, we know that until age twenty-five, the brain is controlled primarily by the limbic system, or our "emotional brain." The section of the brain that is logical does not develop until the late teens or early twenties.

Additionally, there are two time periods of particularly strong brain growth, which send our little ones (or not so little ones!) into emotional turmoil: the toddler years and the teenage years. Since kids at these ages are working in a significantly magnified emotional state, we as their parents need to consider this when we feel that they are acting irrationally. This does not make their irrational reaction okay; it just makes it understandable, and should affect the way that we respond.

Take toddlers as the example: when they do not get what they want, they bite and hit. It does not make it okay, but as adults we know that this is the time period for these typical reactions, so we need to be prepared to handle it. This should work the same with teenagers. When something goes wrong, they are often emotionally explosive and, frankly, often obnoxious. It does not mean that it is okay; we just know that this is the stage where they are, so we need to be prepared to teach them how to handle it.

Children, especially preschoolers and teens, are also testing their independence. They are in a constant struggle between wanting independence and needing their parents. Specifically:

- PRESCHOOLERS are transitioning from complete adult control to some independence. It is the time that they are realizing that they are actually separate beings from their parents, and they have control over their own bodies.

◆ TEENAGERS are also in a particularly difficult stage, testing a completely new realm of independence. They need to test their ability to make decisions and have control over who they are and what they will become. They need to test the boundaries of this newfound independence.

It is important to remember that we are dealing with beings of heightened emotions that are in constant struggle between their desire for independence and their need for parental support. Taking it a step further, it is also essential to recognize that we, too, are also probably dealing with intensified emotions and a struggle for control. After all, there is nothing that can push our own hot buttons like our children—particularly when they are challenging our authority.

Do you see the problem? When humans are emotional, they say and do things that they regret. Remember that anger fuels anger and the need for control leads to deadlock. This is where triggerscripts come in.

◆◆◆

Chapter Eight

Triggerscripts: Avoid Train Wrecks and Direct Your Kids on to the Right Track

So often, parenting is a train wreck just waiting to happen. As parents, we are busy and often overtired. When arguments with our children start, it builds the pressure we already feel. We and our children react like trains accelerating down the tracks and running head-on towards one another. Does the following scenario sound familiar?

> *Child #1:* Mom, I was using that, and Steven just took it out of my hands!
>
> *Child #2:* No, I didn't! I had it, and I was using it before she came over here.
>
> *Parent (in a warning tone):* Guys, I'm on the phone.
>
> *Child #1:* I had it before he did—I was in the middle of using it . . .
>
> *Child #2:* You did not! I had it, and put it down to go to the bathroom, and you took it!
>
> *Child #1:* It was just lying there when I came in—I WANT IT BACK—YOU GRABBED IT FROM ME!

Parent (hollering): I SAID, 'I AM ON THE PHONE!!!' GIVE ME THAT THING! NOW BOTH OF YOU, GET OUT OF HERE!!!!

When the eventual crash happens, we feel badly. After reading Chapter Two (page 29), you now know why we crashed—the control center in our brain was kidnapped, and we reacted impulsively rather than objectively—but that doesn't make us feel any better. How much better it would be to stop the train wreck—provide a signal to the parties involved to change tracks—*before it happens.* That is what a triggerscript does.

A **triggerscript** is *a short script that can trigger a brain pathway to set in motion specific actions.* Triggerscripts can be used to automatically trigger a specific response—usually, a way to escape the situation until we are better able to handle it. Remember, when we are faced with danger or high emotions, the amygdala hijacks the control center in our brains, and we are left with a "fight or flight" response. A triggerscript provides *direction*—a very efficient direction—particularly in situation chockfull of emotional stress.

> *Triggerscripts can be used to automatically trigger a specific response.*

The beauty of triggerscripts is that *through our usage of them, we can teach our children at a young age to respond to them, thereby diffusing so many of the emotional conflicts that are a hallmark of parent/child relationships. We then can also teach our kids to use triggerscripts independently, which can help them as they become more vulnerable to situations involving risk during those 'heavy construction' years (see the previous chapter).* As a result, triggerscripts are a powerful parenting tool.

Do you remember that commercial? Two all-beef patties . . . .

The idea of triggerscripts comes from a wonderful book on branding, *The Microscript Rules: It's Not what people hear. It's what they repeat...*, written by Bill Schley. Microscripts work in marketing in the same way that triggerscripts work in parenting—they create automatic brain pathways.

Let's try a little exercise from his book. Read the following phrases:

- *It melts in your mouth, not.....*
- *If the glove fits, you must....*
- *Stop, drop, and....*
- *No pain, no...*
- *You snooze, you...*

What happened? Did your thinking stop at the end of the phrase, or did *your brain keep going to automatically finish these common phrases?* We bet, if you are like most people, your brain finished the phrase. This is called *audiation.* Audiation is *a brain process that continues a pathway because it is well-cleared and now has become automatic.*

Technically, audiation is a musical term: *the process of mentally hearing music, even when there is no sound.* To try this, turn on one of your favorite songs, and then turn it off part-way through. What happens? You keep hearing the music in your brain. That is audiation: your brain continues down the pathway, even once the song is turned off.

Audiation demonstrates what we have said about brain development—we can reinforce specific thought pathways until they become

> *Audiation is a brain process that continues a pathway because it is well-cleared and now has become automatic.*

automatic. *The goal of a triggerscript is to create a pathway that is automatic, one that triggers a behavior without having to think about it.*

Remember, also, what we said about brain pathways? How the more and more you travel down a pathway, the more it is reinforced? Well, that is how and why triggerscripts work. Scripting is not an easy fix. It takes consistency and hard work. It takes follow-through. It takes being proactive. Triggerscripts require the most consistent work, but offer great potential benefit.

Short but Efficient Direction

Triggerscripts are directive. Triggerscripts are geared toward creating *self-regulatory* behaviors in kids—having them do what they should be doing. If used consistently, triggerscripts teach kids to be able to regulate their own behavior.

When children are young, triggerscripts are used for situations that are repeated time and again—when you want to send a message that is very generalizable. *The shorter and more consistent a script you create for those instances, the more quickly your kids are going to be able to access those automatic brain pathways and set actions into motion.*

Here are a few examples of how triggerscripts can get kids to do what they should be doing:

FIND PATIENCE

Kids have needs. Lots of needs. And they want them met. Now. So *patience* is a quality that has to be learned. And when our kids don't display patience, parents often get frustrated—generating a perfect situation for a parenting train wreck. The answer? *Create and use a triggerscript.*

The children's book *My Jack-O-Lantern* by Nancy Skarmeas, is about a child who visits his grandfather's farm and needs to wait months before his pumpkin grows and becomes a jack-o-lantern. Each time the child asks when the pumpkin is going to become a jack-o-lantern, there is a line in the book: "Be patient, said Grampy." This is a perfect triggerscript for teaching the quality art of patience!

After you have repeated and highlighted this phrase through the reading of the book, start using the line with your kids. When your children are being impatient, say, "Be patient . . . ." and have them finish with ". . . said Grampy" until eventually, in trying times, you only utter, "Be . . . ," and your children come forth with the word "patient" for themselves. The very word "be. . ." is a trigger for them now! It gets them to stop in their tracks and head down a different path—one that has them waiting patiently.

ACT LOGICALLY
(INSTEAD OF STRIKING OUT EMOTIONALLY AT A SIBLING)

Nothing can rile parents quite as much as listening to bickering between their children. It sends our brains right into emotional over-load! It's the perfect situation to create a triggerscript as an antidote.

One triggerscript that we have found very effective is this one: "Spiral up!" Why? Bickering often occurs with one hurt feeling, and spirals down from there. One person's feelings are hurt, so they lash out at another, who lashes out in return. It is a "spiraling-down" effect. Explain to your child that the way to end that downward spiral is to spiral *up*—where one person stops and does or says something nice instead. That begins a new pattern. Once you explain this, the script you need from then on is the "spiral up!" If you use it often enough, it becomes a triggerscript—stopping children in their tracks and sending them on the different path.

TAKE A TIME-OUT TO REGROUP

We have learned that when we are in an emotional state, it hijacks our prefrontal cortex, or our ability to self-regulate. This means that in an emotional situation, none of the players, adults or children, have a great hold on logical thinking. How do we get it back? We remove ourselves from the situation for a short period of time.

This is really what the original "time-out" was for. Unfortunately, as it has become more punitive, it has lost some of its value. Space to escape should be just that—*a space to go to escape from the situation in order to get oneself back under rational control.* In situations where stepping away is essential, it is best to chose a triggerscript that gives explicit direction, such as, "Go sit on the steps."

Before you use this type of triggerscript for the first time, prepare your kids so they understand what it means. Tell them, "It is a place to go to get your thoughts under control. When you are ready to talk, come say to me, 'I'm ready.'" In other words, give your kids some power here—the power to come back. And sure enough, when children can request this calmly, they are usually ready to come back and talk rationally.

These are just three examples of triggerscripts for situations that we know can be generalized. As parents, you know that there are many more scenarios for which you would love your children to self-regulate. The great part about triggerscripts is that you can create them as they are needed. When you find yourself getting frustrated with the same scenario over and over again, create a triggerscript. *The Microscripting Rules* does an excellent job of demonstrating step-by-step why and how to create these short phrases, and we highly recommend reading it. In the meantime, here are some basic guidelines:

Guidelines for Generating Your Own TriggerScripts

TS (TRIGGERSCRIPT) POINT #1-

Use words that tell your children what to do.
It is best to forge a pathway of what kids *should* do, not what they *should not* do. Parents are forever saying, "Don't" and "No," but this does not help the child develop a pathway of thinking for what he *should be* doing, just what he should not. As we've mentioned, triggerscripts should be *directive*—the words that make up these scripts need to give your kids some direction in an emotional time. Remember, the train is running at high speed—you need to send the signal to get on a new path, and quickly.

Here's an example. Janice's two-year-old would hit other children when he wanted something that someone else had. Every time her child would hit someone, she would tell him, "We don't hit," and give her son a time-out. She was being very consistent, but her approach was not changing her son's behavior.

It is wonderful that she was consistent, but Janice was telling her child what *not* to do, and she was not providing him with an alternative of what *to* do! Instead, she needed to model several times what he *could* do through scripting, and then she create a triggerscript, such as, *"You need to ask."* Eventually, she would just start the phrase, allowing her child to fill in the "ask" at the appropriate time. *If she has scripted the situation, this will "trigger" him to know what to do.*

TS POINT #2:

Give any script a rhythmic beat.

A consistent tone reinforces the pathways in our brains. For example, in "Music Together," teachers signal to children that it is time to clean up the instruments by singing "A-way," with a strong emphasis on the first syllable and a note change between the first and second syllable. As soon as the teacher sings the word, the children begin to clean up. The song triggers their brains into action. With young children, triggerscripts prove most effective when parents use a consistent tone, or a rhythmic beat. It is also helpful if *there is a strong pause between the first part of the script ("You need to . . .") and the second half ("ask"),* because eventually, the youngster should be filling in the second half of the triggerscript.

TS POINT #3:

Repeat, repeat, repeat.

Triggerscripts work due to *repetition.* Therefore, they should be used for situations that are *generalizable.* Create them for situations that you are constantly addressing (sharing, patience, bickering between siblings) or for ones that pose a safety risk (wearing bike helmets, diving in the shallow end of the pool, crossing a road). Then use them—again, and again, and again. And again.

TS POINT #4:

Be consistent.

It is helpful if primary caregivers are consistent across the board with their use of triggerscripts. If there is a triggerscript that works, share it with a spouse or teacher, so that it might be reinforced in several different situations. The more times the child hears the triggerscript, the more it clears the pathway in her brain for responding automatically with appropriate behavior.

"Change Tracks:" Stop, Drop, and Roll!

The ultimate goal of triggerscipts is *self-regulation*— teaching kids the tools to control their own behavior. Ideally, we arm them with triggerscripts so that they can act appropriately and safely when we are *not* around. We want them to have triggers that tell them what to do when they are faced with challenges, triggers that automatically send them down the right path.

In most challenging situations, the thought process is blocked and the rational part of our brain is inaccessible. During these times, we want our kids to just *act*. We don't want them to have to think; we want them to just be able to react, just like "stop, drop, and roll" will get them to react if they are ever on fire.

The first step to developing this self-regulation is *talking to your child about the process.* Children need to be able to evaluate and control their own behavior. So explain to your children how they feel emotion in their bodies. Some kids may feel a tightening of the stomach, or experience sweaty palms. Others may report

> *The ultimate goal of triggerscipts is self-regulation*

a "building pressure" in their bodies; this is because often, when we are emotional, the heart rate increases and we literally can feel the pressure rising inside.

Second, *work with your kids to find a triggerscript that helps them know when they need to escape their emotions so they can cool off and use their thinking brains.* At the beginning of the chapter, we introduced a metaphor that can be highly effective in explaining how emotions can affect your response. Children may feel pressure rising inside their bodies like the steam rising up out of the train's chute, which can fuel it faster as it moves toward a crash. *If you use this metaphor of the train with your child, we suggest this triggerscript: "Change tracks."* "Change tracks" means *to do something else to stop that emotion rising:* *move away, redirect, leave the situation, or take time out and come back after things have cooled down.* All this has to be talked about *before* emotion takes charge so your children can recognize the triggerscript as a reminder to escape when emotion starts rising. Just like with any other skill, the ability to self-regulate improves . . . with scaffolding.

> *[The train-wreck metaphor] has to be talked about before emotion takes charge so your children can recognize the triggerscript as a reminder to escape when emotion starts rising.*

Full Steam Ahead to Guided Scripting

As we've mentioned, triggerscripts are a very special type of script: fast, efficient, and directive. They are specifically designed to avoid the train wreck and get us on the right track. Now we turn to a more traditional scripting process, one which draws upon the basic scripting technique (see Chapter Seven) to address the various challenges that parents might guide their children through.

Chapter Nine

Reasonable Requests: Making and Responding to Them

Remember the two basic steps of scripting? Let's review:

STEP 1- CREATE THE SCRIPT.

STEP 2- REPEAT THE ENTIRE PHRASE EXACTLY.

Triggerscripts are a little bit different—they are directive. Most scripts are guided, which means that the adult's job is to scaffold the challenge and guide an appropriate solution. For most situations, there is not a "quick-fix" that will solve the problem. It takes time and creativity to guide the problem-solving process. This is where scripting comes in. In the next few chapters, we provide guidance about how to script these challenges—from the most basic to the more complex.

> *It takes time and creativity to guide the problem-solving process.*

The most basic type of scripting involves *requests*—both making them and responding to them. By "making requests," we mean teaching our children to make a request for something that they want in a polite manner with a reasonable tone. By "responding to requests," we mean teaching our kids to respond to requests made by others in a reasonable manner.

So much of social interaction is based on making and responding to requests, and so often people (both adults and children) don't do either reasonably—which leads to a significant number of headaches! Learning how to handle requests, therefore, forms a foundation for successful social interaction—and also a foundation for resilience. In this chapter, we show you how you can script requests for your child at each stage of their development.

Here are a few examples at each stage:

MAKING REQUESTS:

- ☺ *Toddler/ preschooler:* Mommy, can you please help me get my shoes on?

- ✎ *Elementary-age child:* Mom, could you please sign me up for after-school games this week?

- 🖱 *Tween:* Mom, can I please have a sleepover at Jenna's house this weekend?

- 🎓 *Teen:* Mom, can I please borrow the car on Friday night?

RESPONDING TO REQUESTS:

- ☺ *Toddler/ preschooler (when asked to come to dinner):* Okay—coming!

Elementary-age child (when asked to put away laundry): Okay, Mom, I'll be right there.

 Tween (when asked to turn off video game): I am almost finished with this level—is it okay if I finish it up?

Teen (when asked to clear the kitchen): No problem!

Does this sound too perfect? Of course it does. It won't happen like that all of the time, but if we script out the ideal, eventually those are the pathways that become cleared in our children's brain. *If we give them a chance to practice saying what we would like them to, their brains get trained to do it that way.* Relatively exciting, right?

Fortunately, many times, the requests of our children

> If we give children a chance to practice saying what we would like them to say, their brains get trained to do it that way.

are pretty straightforward. All we have to do is then just follow the two-step scripting process we've learned (pages 78-80), have our kids repeat the request, and move on.

Making Requests

Much of parenting is based on meeting our children's needs. That can certainly be frustrating, but it becomes a lot *less* frustrating if our children learn to ask and respond reasonably! So let our process here be to provide our kids with scripts of how we would like them to ask for things. When a child is very young—at a time before they can even make words—you can start the scripting process by just modeling the appropriate language:

"You would like a bottle? Say, may I have a bottle, please? *Bottle, please.*"

Clearly, your child is not going to be able to say these words yet, but by hearing them, the neural pathway is being started in his or her brain. So, in the beginning, just expect your child to listen to what you say. After that, expect "bottle, please" to be the first phrase that your child will say—it's a watered-down version of the full path. Eventually your child will say a part of the phrase, and finally, the complete phrase. Each time, however, you should provide *the entire phrase first*, so that the child gets to hear the entire pathway. Let's examine a few more examples of age-appropriate scripting requests, and see how we can script appropriate ways for them to get those needs met.

☺ TODDLERS/ PRESCHOOLERS:

Adult: Please don't reach over me to get the bread. Please say, "Mom, could you please pass the bread?"

Child: Mom, could you please pass the bread?

✎ ELEMENTARY-AGE STUDENTS:

Adult: Please don't climb on the chair. Can you say, "Dad, can you help me get this down, please?"

Child: Dad, can you help me get this down please?

🖱 TWEENS:

Child: I need materials for a project at school.

Adult: Can you say, "Mom, would you please take me to the store to get some materials for a school project?"

Child: Mom, can you please take me to the store to get some materials for a school project?

☞ HIGH SCHOOL STUDENTS:

Adult: I know you are upset that you couldn't go out with your friends tonight. Instead of sulking, can you please say, "Mom, I'm really upset that I couldn't go out tonight. If I finish the project tonight, can I please go to the movies tomorrow night with Tess?"

Child: Mom, I'm really upset that I couldn't go out tonight. If I finish the project tonight, can I please go to the movies tomorrow night with Tess?

The examples are endless. Most of the time, kids are happy to repeat the phrase, as they come to realize that if they ask appropriately, they are more likely to get what they need. As their parents, we are much happier to help them out when they ask appropriately.

If it seems simple, that's because, generally, it is. *When kids can communicate their wants and needs, it makes them feel like they are in control.* Many of the problems that lead to control battles with kids or significant others are really a lack of communication or of not knowing the words they need to tell us what they want. If we give them another option, they learn that they have control. They have an appropriate way to meet their needs.

> *When kids can communicate their wants and needs, it makes them feel like they are in control.*

So what are the lessons that our kids have learned about the Four Ss?

1- SELF: *I have the power to get what I need.*

2- SITUATION: *This is a small challenge.*

3- SUPPORT: *I can use my words to ask for help.*

4- STRATEGIES: *I know the strategy to get what I want. If I am polite, people are more likely to want to meet my needs.*

One important point here: *it is extremely important to set limits and be able to say "no" to requests.* Many parents these days want their kids to "like" them, and so they are afraid to set limits. It is helpful to keep in mind that *kids need limits to feel safe.* We are here to parent them, not just be their friends.

When we are saying "no," however, we need to be very aware of the reasons, particularly as our children get older and social capital becomes important. *Social capital* refers to *something that will help kids gain a bit of status in a given situation.* We must be careful not to underestimate the importance of peer relationships when it comes to elementary-, middle-, and high-school students.

Many times, the things that bring social capital as kids get older are the items that send parents into a panic—violent video games, cell phones, sexy clothes. We are not advocating for these items—in fact, their ownership often creates more social problems than they solve— but when an adolescent says, "But Mom, *everyone* has these. Nobody will like me if I don't get them," we need to at least listen and respond reasonably to our child's worry and concern. For some items, we may choose to set a strict limit in the name of safety, but for others, we might consider that it may not be all that bad to give in (as long as it does not compromise our children's safety in any way). In instances when we do decide to give in, it is important to explain why.

☞ Here is a script to use with older kids when it comes to listening to their requests that involve the issue of social capital:

Gail: Mom, I am supposed to go out after school with Helen on Friday. Everybody at school goes out in the afternoon with their Uggs on, so I am not going unless I get them. I always look so stupid without them, and everyone makes fun of me when I wear my regular shoes. I don't want to go.

Adult: I hear you saying that everyone else has Uggs, and you need to get them to feel accepted in school. Instead of threatening, can you reword that and say, "Mom, everyone else at school has Uggs and I really want to get them?"

Gail: Mom, everyone else at school has Uggs, and I really want to get them.

Adult: I understand you want to get them because everyone has them. I want you to understand, however, that your real friends will like you whether or not you have "Uggs." I think that Uggs are fine and have no problem with you wearing them, so yes, you can get Uggs. But they are expensive, so we need to work out a plan for how you can help to buy them. If they are that important to you, let's work out a plan together.

☞ This scenario also provides you with the framework for when "yes" will not be the answer and you need to set very specific limits:

Adult: Gail, you cannot wear that shirt to school. It is too tight and too short. You need to go find something else.

Gail: But Mom, everyone wears shirts like this.

Adult: I understand, and there are times—like with the Uggs—that I will say "yes" because it helps you feel comfortable, but I do not like you wearing shirts like that to school. I think that they are inappropriate, so you need to go upstairs and change.

Gail: But everyone will make fun of me.

Adult: If they make fun of you, you can say, "My mom is such a pain. She won't let me wear my favorite shirt to school." I am happy to take the blame, but you may not wear that to school.

Our children need to be able to say to their friends, "My mom won't let me." It gives them a safety net—so script it for them.

Responding Appropriately

Now let's turn to responding to a request made by someone else. Our goal here is to get our kids to respond reasonably and politely.

Interestingly, the first challenge here is getting kids to respond at all! Often, they don't respond. There are two reasons for this: 1) they don't really think that a response is required (unintentional); or 2) they do not want to respond because they think that it will require them to do something that they don't want to do. Let's look at each reason:

◆ UNINTENTIONAL. In the first case, it is usually a matter of a question being asked to a general audience, so the child assumes that no response on their part is requested. For example, we might ask, "What would you guys like for breakfast?" or "Would anyone like some orange juice?" So often, adult voices become white noise to kids—they hear us, but it doesn't really register. It is not that they are trying to ignore us, but they don't really think about how frustrating it is for us to not get a response. In those cases, it usually works to just say, "It is frustrating when I ask something and you don't respond. Could you just give a response, even if it is, "I'm not hungry right now, Mom, so I don't really want any breakfast." Many times, they are just assuming that someone else might respond, so it is important to let them know that it is each person's responsibility.

◆ REQUIRING THEM TO DO SOMETHING THEY DON'T WANT TO DO. In the second case, kids don't respond because they do not know any strategies to respond in a way that they can get their own needs met. Let's look at an example:

Adult: Dinner is ready.
Child (silent):
Adult: Dinner is ready.
Child (silent):
Adult (Fuming by now): I said DINNER IS READY!!!!

Let's analyze: the chances are, if he heard you, he is in the middle of something (playing, television-watching, video-gaming), so he either is not registering your request or he is not responding because he doesn't want to stop what he is doing. It is time to do a little scripting.

Here is one option:
Adult: It is frustrating when you don't answer when I call.
 Can you say, "Mom, I'll be right there?"
Child: Mom, I'll be right there.

Now, here's what to do if your child is not answering because he's involved in an activity. First, before we script, we need to remember that *we too need to make our requests reasonable!* Most adults do not get off the phone right away when their children call over to them, so it is not reasonable to ask children to transition immediately either. We need to give them words for how to respond to us (meeting our needs) while still being able to find a reasonable place to transition (meeting their needs too).

How many of us can think of a time when we were getting incredibly frustrated when calling our child in to brush his teeth because he didn't answer? Well, often isn't part of the problem the fact that we were standing at the bathroom sink wondering where he was? By explaining to our child that in instances like this, he has the right to request, "Can I just finish up reading this page or shooting this last hoop?" we are creating a pathway for our child that meets everyone's needs. We can use scripting to give our kids the opportunity to offer up *reasonable responses.*

Next, what are we to do to avoid control battles, which happen when we want our child to do something and they either: 1) do not want to do it *when* we want them to do it; or 2) do not want to do it *the way we want them to do it?* Most often, parents take it as an all-or-nothing, when really, compromise is usually the *reasonable* answer—we just need to use scripting to get there. What kids really want is some control in the situation. For example, if dinner is ready and we want them to join us, the following may take place:

> *Adult:* Dinner is ready!
> *Child:* I am not hungry.

As you are most likely the chef in this situation, how are feeling? You may feel tired, having just spent your precious time cooking dinner. Your emotions start to rise and get out of whack because your child is not ready to come to the table—*how dare he not be hungry!* But if you look closely at the situation your child may be engaged in at the moment, you may see some room for negotiation before anger gets the best of you and your good efforts go down the drain. You may notice, for example, that your child is playing a video game. Likely, the "not being hungry" is the only answer that he can think of that will let him continue playing. So let's try some scripting:

> *What kids really want is some control in the situation.*

> *Adult:* Can you say, "I'm just finishing up a level. Can I come when I finish this level?"
>
> *Child:* I'm just finishing up a level. Can I come when I finish this level?

Once a child is given an opportunity to verbalize what he wants, he is likely to respond appropriately and come to the table at the end of the level—for you have made a reasonable request. Your suggestion here also teaches your children that they can tell you the truth during times like these.

So, let's take a look at our framework: what are we teaching about the Four Ss?

How The Four Ss Come Into Play

- ◆ SELF: *My parents listened to me and let me find a good place to stop the game. I can be responsible and keep my end of the bargain.*

- ◆ SITUATION: *When my parents make a request, I can make a reasonable counter-request and they will at least consider it.*

◆ SUPPORT: *I can handle this on my own.*

◆ STRATEGIES: *I can think of a reasonable request to get what I want.*

Okay, so now kids know that they need to respond. Now let's take a look at times when they respond *inappropriately.*

Making Sure a Response is Appropriate: Rewording and Retoning

We need to always remember that *young people are learning language.* They do not naturally know what to say and how to say it, so they experiment. Sometimes they experiment with inappropriate wording, and sometimes they experiment with inappropriate tones.

In the toddler and preschool years, kids experiment with whining, and in the elementary and adolescent years, they experiment with "rude" tones. Remember, this is an experiment. It does not mean that it is acceptable, but it means that we can use these opportunities as *teachable moments instead of reasons to get angry.*

Also, we can understand that the brains of our children are developing at an incredible rate, and each day our kids are going through all sorts of emotional turmoil in their lives. If they are overtired because they have not had a nap or stayed up all night studying, sometimes they end up being rude and disrespectful. That does not mean that it is okay for them to be rude, it just means that we need to recognize the reason and act accordingly. If we just fly off the handle at an inappropriate tone or response, our emotions take over, their emotions take over—and the battle has begun.

To keep a situation under control, it is helpful to think about the way that we feel when we are tired. Sometimes, when we are overtired or upset, we are not reasonable, even as adults. That does not make it okay, but don't we just hope that others recognize that there is a reason and respond accordingly? (For example: "I must admit, I am overtired because I was woken up three times last night. When I am tired, I get upset easily. It would be really helpful if you guys would listen to me without my having to ask five times.").

Now, when kids make requests with inappropriate wording or tones, it is important to set the limit ("You may not whine" or, "You may not speak to me that way"), but it is then important to teach them the right pathway ("You may say..."). Tone is a critical piece of the language pathway, and those pathways that are reinforced will continue. Here are a few examples:

☺ TODDLERS/ PRESCHOOLERS:

Child (whining): I want a cookie!

Adult: You may not whine. You may say in a happier tone, "Mom, may I please have a cookie?"

Child: Mom, may I please have a cookie.

—or—

Child: Arrrggghhhh!!!!

Adult: You may not scream if things aren't working out the way you want them. You may say, "Mom, can you help me put my coat on?"

Child: Mom, can you help me put my coat on?

✎ ELEMENTARY-AGE CHILD:

Adult: Sally, please go upstairs to do your homework.

Sally: I TOLD you already that I don't have any homework tonight!

Adult: You may not speak to me like that. Please say, "Remember I don't have any homework tonight?"

Sally: Remember I don't have any homework tonight?

🖱 TWEENS:

Sam: Can I go over to Eric's house?

Adult: Not tonight. We need to go pick up Jenna.

Sam: You never let me do ANYTHING.

Adult: Please don't talk to me like that. I know you're disappointed, so can you say, "Mom, I really want to go see Eric. Can you try to arrange a time that I can go soon?"

Sam: Mom, I really want to go see Eric. Can you try to arrange a time that I can go soon?

Adult: Sure, honey. I'll give Eric's mom a call later today and set something up.

🎓 TEENS:

Adult: Peter, could you please take out the garbage?

Peter: What are you, blind? I'm right in the middle of putting this project together. If I leave now, it will ruin everything!

Adult: Your words and tone are disrespectful. I expect you to treat me with respect. You can say, "Dad, I'm right in the middle of something. Is it okay if I take the garbage out after I'm finished?"

Peter: Dad, I'm right in the middle of something. Is it okay if I take it out after I'm finished?

Most times, your children will repeat what you say—really. And this teaches them some critical lessons about the Four Ss:

◆ SELF: *My parents are listening to my needs.*

◆ SITUATION: *When I am whiney or rude, I don't get what I want. When I ask appropriately, I have a better chance.*

◆ SUPPORT: *My parents are here to support me.*

◆ STRATEGIES: *If I use appropriate words and a respectful tone, I have a better chance of getting what I want, and my parents will not get angry at me.*

Remember: Kids are smart! They will begin to understand that when they use the words that they are fed, they are much more likely to get things that they want. That doesn't mean that we give them what they want every time they ask appropriately, but they do learn that this approach opens them up to a better negotiating position. Once they have asked appropriately, we can explain why we will or will not do what they asked.

The key to both making and responding to requests, as well as the key to social interaction in general, is being *reasonable.* We want to reinforce for them that if they make reasonable requests and if they respond in a reasonable way, a social interaction will go much more smoothly. But we do need to script for them what it means to be "reasonable."

By providing exact phrasing through scripting, we reinforce particular language pathways. Of course, we are not able to blaze every language pathway for our children. Fortunately (and as mentioned earlier), when they are

> *The key to both making and responding to requests, as well as the key to social interaction in general, is being reasonable.*

given practice in using simple phrases routinely, children develop the fundamental pathways that they need in order to improvise more complex and effective language. When they are given the foundational language for reasonable requests, kids are more likely to be successful negotiating more complex social situations . . . which leads us to the next chapter.

Chapter Ten

Prosocial Interaction: How to Include Others, Share, and Compromise

We are social beings. We are constantly interacting with other people and yet, social language does not always come naturally, smoothly, or fluently.

One reason that social interaction is so difficult? Kids are typically egocentric—they think that everyone can understand what they are thinking, yet have trouble understanding what others are thinking. In order to interact effectively, kids need to be able to understand someone else's perspective and then

One of our jobs as parents is to teach our children to understand other people's perspectives and then help them develop the skills to negotiate a reasonable course of action.

negotiate a compromise. One of our jobs as parents is to teach our children to understand other people's perspectives and then help them develop the skills to negotiate a reasonable course of action. Not an easy task, but it can be done—gradually and repetitively.

There are three themes that we need to teach our children about prosocial interaction, and these involve knowing how to: 1) actively include other people; 2) share objects (food, toys, etc.); and 3) propose compromises about activity choices. You see, *our kids tend to repeat the problems or issues they have in negotiating these situations over and over again. So if we can teach our children strategies to handle those situations, we go a long way in avoiding conflict and helping them feel successful.*

To accomplish this, we need to teach our children: 1) empathy, and 2) strategies for successful negotiation. If we can teach them to understand the way others are feeling and then teach them strategies to negotiate the situation, they will be in a more powerful position socially.

Let's look at how our children can develop prosocial behaviors at each stage of their development:

☺ Toddlers

INCLUDING OTHERS

When children are very young, true social interactions with peers are limited. Before they are of preschool age, children do not typically take part in cooperative play. Usually, kids of this age prefer to play with an object on their own, and do not really care about being "included." So, for example, when they see an object that they want, they want it and don't have patience to wait. Nor are they developmentally ready to initiate and continue social interactions.

Infants and toddlers benefit greatly from exposure to social situations *if adults are there to help them scaffold the interaction and begin to teach them social skills.* Children are typically drawn to other children. They are fascinated with these "other same-sized creatures" but typically, are not adept at engaging with them.

In order to teach toddlers how to interact, it is extremely helpful to literally script their conversations. The adult can provide the language, and then, if they do not have the language needed, the adult can shorten it as much as needed.

So, to encourage a social connection, a parent may try this:

> *Our goal [for toddlers] is to simply get the kids to play near one another, not with one another.*

Adult: Lilly, look. There is a little girl your age. Can you say, "Hi, I'm Lilly? Hi."

Lilly: Hi.

Adult: She is playing with dolls, too. Can you show her your doll and say, "See my doll? See?"

Lilly: See?

Often, our goal here is to simply get the kids to play near one another, not with one another. *Proximity* is the key.

SHARING OBJECTS

Sharing objects is also beyond the understanding of most toddlers, but a reasonable goal for parents to promote is turn-taking. Recently Janine, the mother of a sixteen-month-old, was trying to get her daughter to share a toy. The little girl, Sarah, had the toy, and another child, Sam, wanted it. Her mom said firmly, "You need to share," but Sarah was having no part of it. Well, "sharing" is a very sophisticated concept—something beyond the grasp of this young child at this time. So we suggested to Janine that she teach her daughter how to "take turns" instead. And then, because the other child was older and more used to turn-taking, we asked that child to take very short turns, which we scaffolded. Here is the conversation that ensued:

> *Adult:* Sam, can you say, "Sarah, can I have a turn please?"
> *Sam:* Can I have a turn please?
> *Adult (guiding the toy to Sam):* Sarah, we are going to take turns. Sam's turn, now. Sam's turn. (As soon as Sam got the toy.) Sarah, can you say, "Turn please." Sarah's turn!

And then right away, the adult guided Sam to give the toy to Sarah. We repeated this interaction several times, and eventually, Sarah gave up the toy willingly. It became a game because she knew that she was going to get a turn—and this lesson was much more concrete for Sarah than the idea of sharing.

The lessons in terms of the Four Ss? *Sarah can begin to control getting the toy and giving it to others.*

So often, as parents, when we are playing, we willingly give up any object to our child (providing it's not dangerous) right away. In fact, we often let children take things right out of our hands when they want them. In the long run, this teaches children to grab, which will translate into peer relationships. A peer who experiences grabbing will most likely responds with anger, and this reaction confuses our kids. It's better to practice turn-taking with children as soon as they begin to have *receptive language* (which is, *the ability to understand language even if they don't speak the words yet*).

COMPROMISING ON ACTIVITIES

Turn-taking with activities works similarly to turn-taking with objects. Kids may not be able to fully negotiate a compromise at this age. Their egocentricity can often be dealt with through distraction, and their tolerance for waiting can increase when they understand that their needs ultimately will be met. Therefore, it is helpful to "take turns"—but be sure to let them know that when they complete an activity that they don't want to do, they will be able to do an activity that they want to do. Here is an example:

> *If we assure [toddlers] that their needs/desires will be met, they can be much more "reasonable."*

> *Child (screaming):* My train!!
>
> *Adult:* Can you say, "I want to play with my train? Train, please?"
>
> *Child:* Train, please.
>
> *Adult:* I know that you want to play with your train, but right now we need to brush your teeth. Teeth and then train. Teeth and then train. Please come brush your teeth so you can play with your train.

So often, kids seem "unreasonable" because they do not know what is going to happen. *If we assure them that their needs/ desires will be met, they can be much more "reasonable."*

☺ ✎ Preschoolers/ Early Elementary-Age Children
INCLUDING OTHERS

When children enter preschool (about three to four years old), they start to interact with others more. They develop friendships and preferences for playing with particular children. So, this is the age when they are ready to begin to explore the dynamics of social interactions.

As parents, we want to teach our children the valuable lesson of being empathetic and the important social strategies of including others or asking to be included. At this age, that usually means knowing how to ask someone if they want to play with you, or how to ask if you can play with someone else. There is a big difference between the two—and it has to do with power.

If a child is asking if another child wants to play with him, that child has the power in the social situation, and this affects the requesting and the scripts for children. What we want to teach children at this age is that when they are in the power position, they can proactively check to see if there is anyone that might want to be included, and if they are in the less powerful position, that it is okay to ask to be included.

Here is an example of each strategy:

Adult: There is another child about your age who just got here. Can you say to him, "Hi, my name is Tim. What is your name?"

Tim: Hi, my name is Tim. What is your name?

(other child stares)

Adult (to the other child): What is your name?

Other child: David

Adult: Can you say, "Hi, my name is David?"

David: Hi, my name is David.

Adult (to Tim): Can you say, "Do you want to play with my trains?"

Tim: Do you want to play with my trains?

David: Sure.

In this situation, Tim has the power because he has the trains and he is offering to play with David.

Let's look at the same example, but with Tim asking to be included in the play instead.

> **Adult:** That boy over there is playing with trains all by himself. I bet he might like to play with someone his own age. Can you say to him, "Hi, my name is Tim. What is your name?"
>
> **Tim:** Hi, my name is Tim. What is your name?
>
> *(other child stares)*
>
> **Adult (to the other child):** What is your name?
>
> **Other child:** David.
>
> **Adult:** Can you say, "Hi, my name is David?"
>
> **David:** Hi, my name is David.
>
> **Adult (to Tim):** Can you say, "Can I play trains with you?"
>
> **Tim:** Can I play trains with you?
>
> **David:** Sure.

In this situation, David has the power because he has the trains.

Teacher and early childhood education researcher Vivian Paley wrote an excellent book called, *You Can't Say You Can't Play,* the title of which is a great script to teach kids at this age. However, there is an important follow-up—children need to know *what* they can say rather than just being told what not to say. Up until about third grade, it is usually pretty easy to get kids to include everyone in their play, as long as you show them how it can be done. Notice that in both of these examples the answer David gave was, "Sure." Clearly, that is not always (or even

Children need to know what they can say rather than just being told what not to say.

117

often) the answer that kids give, which leads to more complex scripting. The next chapter will address these situations where we or our children are negotiating conflict.

SHARING

Once a child is of preschool age, they also begin to play cooperatively, so it's a good time to introduce the idea of sharing. Typically, there are "favored toys"—those that a few kids want to play with (usually all at the same time!)—so they need strategies to figure out how to work it all out. The most common ways are taking turns, playing together, and dividing the objects. Here is an example of scripting to teach your kids these social strategies.

> *Adult:* All three of you want to play with the magnets, right?
>
> *Kids:* Yes.
>
> *Adult:* Okay, there are a lot of magnets here. Let's come up with a way that we can all play. I see three different ways. One way that we can do it is to divide up the magnets, and you can each build something. Another way is that you can all build something together, or you can each take turns using all of the magnets.
>
> *Sam:* I want to make a spaceship.
>
> *Adult:* Okay, can you say, "Hey guys, I want to make a spaceship. Do you guys want to build it together?"
>
> *Sam:* Hey guys, I want to build a spaceship. Do you guys want to build it together?
>
> *Ted:* Sure.
>
> *Bill:* No. I want to make a house.
>
> *Adult:* Can you say, "No, thanks. I want to build a house."
>
> *Bill:* No, thanks. I want to build a house.

Adult: Which pieces would you need to build the house?

Bill (points them out): These five.

Adult: Can you say, "Can I take these pieces and build a house, and you guys can have the rest for your spaceship?"

Bill: Can I take these pieces and build a house, and you guys can have the rest for your spaceship?

Ted & Sam: Sure.

Usually, kids at this age are happy to compromise if they have some adult help in doing it. Then, once you teach them these strategies, they can begin to use the scripts, slowly at first and then more competently on their own.

COMPROMISING ON ACTIVITIES

Often our children want to spend their time in different ways. When this occurs, the strategies to use are these: 1) they can decide on one of the activities (one person gives up his choice or find a fair way to choose); 2) they can take turns doing the activity ("first we do one, and then we do the other"); or 3) they can choose a completely different activity. Here is an example of a script to use:

Adult: You can watch a movie as long as you can agree on what you want to see.

Stefan: I want to watch Bob the Builder.

Sarah: I want to watch My Little Pony.

Adult: Okay, we are only watching one movie right now, and you guys need to agree on it. So, here are some options. We can choose one of those movies—maybe by flipping a coin or doing rock, paper, scissors—or one of you could agree that if we do the other person's movie today, we will do your movie next time; or the two of you could come up with a third movie that you both like. Which do you guys want to do?

Stefan: Let's flip a coin.

Adult: Sarah, do you agree?

Sarah: Okay.

Adult: Now, if you agree to that, whichever one of you loses will need to agree to see the other movie. Then the next time, that person will choose. Do you agree to that?

Both: Yes.

(Adult flips the coin—Sarah wins)

Stefan: But I wanted Bob the Builder!

Adult: You agreed to the coin toss, so we are watching My Little Pony today. Can you say, "I really wanted to see Bob the Builder; can we watch that next time?"

Stefan: I really wanted to see Bob the Builder; can we see that next time?

Adult: Yes, we will watch the movie you want to see next time.

The point is that we are teaching children strategies for success in social interactions. If they come up with a different solution that they agree upon, that is a win, but we start with teaching them a few options for scripts that they can draw upon in many situations.

✎ Elementary-School-Age Children

The transition from second to third grade is *huge*. Academically, the focus changes from learning to read to reading to learn. Children who have not learned to read well find themselves struggling. And socially, third grade introduces a much more complex dynamic. This increase in social demands is extremely difficult for some children, and it is a time when it is even more important for parents to

> *Socially, third grade introduces a much more complex dynamic.*

teach successful social interaction strategies. Unfortunately, it is also the time that children begin to be more independent. In elementary school, much of children's social interaction takes place away from parents, removing the immediate opportunity to scaffold at a prime moment in our kids' lives. If we have started the scaffolding early on with our kids, it is extremely helpful because during this stage they can draw upon the strategies that we have already taught them. Otherwise, we need to do much of the scaffolding either *before or after* the social occurrence takes place.

INCLUDING OTHERS

Many times, kids want to include others, but they just don't know how. By talking to kids about the social situations that they are facing at school, parents can script strategies that they might use to include others.

Let's take a look at a few examples. In this first one, the parent is lucky enough to be present, and is able to scaffold in the moment:

> *Adult:* Those kids look like they are having fun. Would you like to play with them?
> *Ashley:* Yes.
> *Adult:* Let's walk over to that little girl, and you say to her, "Can I play with you guys?"

This leaves her vulnerable, so the adult needs to walk over with her and scaffold the interaction—remember, the other little girl will probably not know what to say.

Ashley: Can I play with you, guys?

Girl: No *(this is a worst case scenario—most times they will actually say "sure").*

Adult: This is Ashley, and she really would like to play with you guys. Could you tell me what you are playing?

Girl: House.

Adult: Could we find a role for Ashley?

Girl: We already have a mommy and two sisters.

Adult: Could she be a friend or cousin, and you are having her over for a playdate?

Girl: Okay.

Adult: Could you say, "You can play—how about you are the friend who is over for a playdate?"

Girl: You can play—how about you are the friend who is over for a playdate?

Ashley: Okay.

Adult: Ashley, can you say, "Can you introduce me to your friends?"

Ashley: Can you introduce me to your friends?

Adult: What are your names?

Girl: Sally is the mom, and Debbie and me are the sisters.

Adult: And what is your name?

Girl: Katie.

Adult: Can you say, "Sally and Debbie, this is Ashley; she is going to play with us. She is going to be the friend who comes over for a playdate."

Now this may seem like a lot of work for a simple interaction, but it is really important to begin to look at why this is so critical. At this age, "You can't say, 'You can't play'" doesn't work very well! If we tell kids that when someone asks them to play they can't say "no," then we are not teaching social skills, we are merely teaching that the adults are in control of their play. Working through the situation and trying to understand where the "no" comes from is much more helpful. Often the "no" comes from a child's inability to think through and understand how they can include someone else (in this instance, Ashley becomes the friend who is arriving at the house for a playdate). Once they see that they can do it, they are often happy to include another child in the group's play.

Sometimes kids also refuse to allow another child in when it is a matter of timing ("we are right in the middle of a game right now, but you can play the next game"). But whatever the scenario, the experience of realizing that *they* can have the control is extremely important. There are certainly times that we need to intervene and prevent exclusion, but a better solution is to teach our kids negotiating skills they need to reduce their reliance on parent/adult intervention. As a lesson, this provides them with so much more!

> *Whenever possible, you want to give children the power to control their own play, offering help for them only when it comes to learning the skills to do it appropriately.*

"You can't say, 'You can't play,'" doesn't teach them about their own ability to control the play, the ability to navigate the situation in the future, and the strategies that they can use to include or be included. Whenever possible, you want to *give children the power* to control their own play, offering help for them only when it comes to learning the skills to do it appropriately. In this sample interaction, all of the kids' responses were respected, and they had input as it developed.

Now let's look at an example that is happening at school, a time when scaffolding cannot be offered by the parent "in the moment."

Adult: Meg, how are things going at school?

Meg: Great. Fourth grade's the best!

Adult: Who are you hanging out with at recess these days?

Meg: Mostly Jenna and Amrit. We all like to go on the swings together.

Adult: How is Sarah doing?

Meg: You mean the new girl?

Adult: Yes.

Meg: I don't know.

Adult: Who does she hang out with at recess?

Meg: I'm not sure. I don't really see her with anyone.

Adult: How do you think she feels about that?

Meg: I don't know.

Adult: You know, it is really hard to be the new person at school. Have you ever tried to ask if she wants to play with you and Jenna and Amrit?

Meg: No. But we would let her play if she asked.

Adult: I know you would, and I am glad about that. But sometimes, it is really hard if you are the new person. It is a lot easier for you to ask her to play than it is for her to ask you if she can play. So can you try something new? Can you just keep a eye out, and if she looks like she isn't playing with someone else, can you go to her and say, "Hey, Sarah, do you want to come swing on the swings with us?"

Meg: Okay.

It seems like such a simple thing, but many kids don't think like this! They need to be reminded to invite others to play, and they need to be given specific wording about how to do it. It is particularly important for "popular" kids to learn how to include others, because they have the "social capital" to make it work, and others will follow their example. A key to great prosocial interaction (besides compromise and empathy) is *consideration*—having kids actively begin to think about how they can be considerate of others' feelings.

SHARING

As kids hit their preteen years, they begin to be more interested in privacy. Along with that privacy, they begin to be more concerned about their own possessions. They understand more about the concept of including others and sharing, but they need to learn a more sophisticated understanding of how to share, or not share, their possessions.

There are very few cut-and-dry decisions about sharing. Is it okay for pre-teens to have a diary and expect that nobody—including parents—should have

> *The important point to remember is that kids need to learn how to handle these decisions—and you can teach them through scripting.*

access? In this era of technology, can they have their own Facebook page? Do we need to respect their interest in not wanting to share specific things with friends and siblings? Which objects are those? Where should you draw the line?

Each family needs to make their own decisions here. The important point to remember is that kids need to learn how to handle these decisions—and you can teach them through scripting.

> *Adult:* Sarah, I know that Kelly is coming over today. The last time she was over, you got upset because she broke one of your favorite necklaces. What do you think you can do to avoid something like that happening again?
>
> *Sarah:* I don't know. I know Kelly loves to try on jewelry.
>
> *Adult:* I think it is great that you guys like to try on jewelry, but there are some pieces that are more fragile than others that have a lot of meaning for you. I know that Kelly would never want to break something that meant a lot to you.
>
> *Sarah:* Maybe I could take my favorite necklaces and put them away so they won't get broken.
>
> *Adult:* What if Kelly asks about them?
>
> *Sarah:* I don't know.
>
> *Adult:* You could tell her that you love sharing the necklaces with her but those two mean a lot to you, so you don't want to take them out.
>
> *Sarah:* Okay.

For things that are not particularly precious, we want to encourage sharing.

> *Adult:* We are going to see the Smiths today. You know that Robert loves Legos. Why don't you bring that new set that you got to show him?

Mark: No. Sam always wants to play with us when I bring Legos.

Adult: What do you think you could do so that you can share with both Robert and Sam?

Mark: I don't know.

Adult: Maybe you could say "Hey, Sam, I brought you some Legos to play with. Can you try to build a space ship while Robert and I put this set together? Then we can show you how it works."

Robert: Yeah, I guess I could do that.

Just like including others, sharing is a matter of thinking ahead and trying to be creative about solutions.

COMPROMISING ON ACTIVITIES

The funny thing about preteens is the difficulty that they have distinguishing between what they feel and what is truly happening. Often, if they want to do something and a friend wants to do something else, they interpret the situation as social rejection—you don't want to do what I want to do, therefore, you don't want to be with me.

The solution, once again, is to be creative, and to teach them that feelings are just as important as the activity itself.

Adult: What's wrong?

Jennifer: Rebecca never wants to be with me.

Adult: What makes you think that?

Jennifer: Today at school, I asked her to go on the swings at recess, but she said "no." Then after school, I asked her to sit with me and she didn't want to.

Adult: What did she do after you asked her to swing?

Jennifer: She went to the slide with Debbie.

Adult: What did she do after school?

Jennifer: She went into the gym.

Adult: Did you ask if you could join her?

Jennifer: No, I didn't want to go to the gym.

Adult: Do you think that maybe she didn't want to slide or sit down? It might not be a matter of her not wanting to be with you, just that she wanted to do something else. If you want to spend time with Rebecca, maybe you could talk to her and say, "Hey Rebecca, I would like to do something with you. Can we try to find something that we both want to do?"

Tweens/Teens

As kids get older, the social interactions get more complex—and the stakes get higher. Middle- and high-school students pretty much live for positive social interactions, but with emotions running high they are hyper-aware of the potential social pitfalls. When our children are adolescents, it's the rare time when we can script a conversation for them as an event or dialogue is happening. Therefore, we often need to do the scripting ahead of time—which means that we need to *predict the types of situations that they might encounter.*

Hopefully, by this point in their lives, your tweens and/or teens will have gained the fundamental skills of how to negotiate activities, include people, and share objects, and the scripting you offer will merely be reminders to include others, take turns, or share. The point is *balance*—we want our kids to learn to stick up for themselves, while still being considerate of other's feelings. We want them to have the strategies to propose and negotiate compromises. The sooner we teach those strategies the sooner they will use

> *We want [our kids] to learn to stick up for themselves, while still being considerate of other's feelings.*

them throughout their lives. Here are some examples for teens:

INCLUDING OTHERS

Jose: Mom, can I go to the movies Friday night with Marco and Nick?

Adult: Who's driving?

Jose: I was hoping that I could take the car. We planned to meet there, because they are both driving.

Adult: You can take the car as long as you get back here by midnight.

Jose: Great—thanks!

Adult: Jose, why isn't Sam going with you guys? He's pretty much always a part of the mix.

Jose: He can't go because he doesn't have a ride.

Adult: Do you think he would want to go?

Jose: Well, yeah, probably.

Adult: Why don't you offer him a ride?

Jose: I didn't think you would let me.

Adult: I want you to help your friends out—so it is always worth asking something like, 'Hey, Mom, can I offer Sam a ride?'

Jose: Can I?

Adult: Yes—why don't you call and ask him?

SHARING

Adult: Greg, aren't you staying after school with a bunch of kids to study this afternoon?

Greg: Yeah.

Adult: Why don't you bring a bag of pretzels and a box of granola bars so that you guys can have a snack while you are studying?

Greg: Okay—good idea.

COMPROMISING ON ACTIVITIES

Adult: I thought you and Rachel were going shopping this afternoon.

Katie: She didn't want to go.

Adult: I thought you wanted her opinion about that shirt you were thinking of buying.

Katie: Yeah, but she said she couldn't go.

Adult: Did you tell her you wanted her help?

Katie: No.

Adult: Why don't you give her a call and say, "Hey Rachel, I know that you couldn't go shopping today, but there is something I really want to show you. Could we find a time that we can go together?"

Katie: I guess I could do that.

Prosocial Interaction . . . Proactive Thinking

Prosocial interaction is usually a matter of teaching kids to be proactive in their thinking. Kids are often willing to be prosocial, but they either don't think about it or they don't know how to do it. Our goal as parents is to scaffold situations so that our children begin to recognize when they can be prosocial—including others, sharing, and compromising—and know how to do it.

Now let's take a look at how to handle situations when it doesn't quite go as planned....

Chapter Eleven

It's a Win-Win: Helping Kids Negotiate and Resolve Conflicts

Inevitably, with social interaction comes conflict. It is natural, but that doesn't make it any less frustrating or upsetting! Whenever we get more than two people together, there is a chance for problems: arguments, exclusion, gossiping, etc. Sometimes, kids can work things out on their own. Sometimes, they cannot come up with a creative, alternate strategy, so they need a little help. In this chapter, we address those times when our kids need help negotiating creative solutions.

A Chance to Learn

As hard as it may be, it is best to look at conflict as opportunity for learning. When children are faced with an opinion that is different than theirs, it stretches and forces them to become a little less ego-centric. We need to remember, however, that this does not neces-

> *It is best to look at conflict as opportunity for learning*

sarily come easily (just as it may not always come easily for us). Young children often cannot even understand or comprehend someone else's point-of-view, and that is why we need to scaffold for them.

There are three important stages to successful conflict resolution:

◆ Cooling off;

◆ Resolving the conflict; and

◆ Crafting apologies.

Let's take a look at each stage.

Stage 1- COOLING OFF

The first stage of conflict resolution is *making sure that person in the conflict is cooled off.* Many times, the key to resolving a conflict is *timing*—taking the time to make sure that each side is calm before negotiating begins.

When we are in a "non-emotional" or objective state of mind, it is extremely difficult to understand the perspective of someone who is in the exact opposite "emotional" state of mind. As adults, we tend to underestimate the importance of things in our children's lives and why they get so upset and angry.

It is helpful to remind yourself at these times that children are so emotional because their brains are primarily run by the limbic system, which is based on emotion (as opposed to adults who have the control center in place to temper emotions). This is their natural state. It is often also beneficial to recognize that we, too, get emotional about silly things—like a slow driver in front slowing us down—that in the long run are no more important than the things that we scoff at when our kids get angry or upset.

Let's face it, when our children or we are emotional, *we can become irrational. We do and say things that we do not mean.* So if our children are in a conflict and wearing out-of-control emotions on their sleeve, the first thing that we need to do is remove them from the situation to let them calm down. In many ways, it is one of the greatest gifts that we can give them. Hopefully we can remove them before they have done or said something that they will regret.

The problem is, when children are emotional or irrational, it can be difficult to get them to extract themselves. The solution *is to prepare them ahead of time with a triggerscript (remember Chapter Eight?) to remove them from the situation.*

This triggerscript may stay the same through the years, or it may gradually change as kids get older. The important part is that it is a short phrase that directs someone away from the situation ("Go sit down on the steps") to have some cool-down time.

Stage 2- RESOLVING THE CONFLICT

The next step to conflict resolution is *scaffolding the resolution of the conflict—or trying to draw out each perspective and scripting a negotiation between the two parties.* The key job of adults is to scaffold the *negotiation*—not direct the resolution.

> **The key job of adults is to scaffold the negotiation— not direct the resolution.**

As our children age, the types of conflicts that they experience and the kinds of successful resolutions change dramatically. Once again, we address this material through children's developmental stages.

☺ BABIES/ TODDLERS

Babies and toddlers are impulsive and egocentric: if they want something, they will take it. If you take it away, they will probably cry. This presents a problem when they grab their sibling's toys (which they find more interesting than anything else).

At this beginning stage of your children's lives, often the best course of action is *to teach any older child in your family or at play to trade.* For example:

> **Sam:** Rich (Sam's little brother) just grabbed my truck!
> **Adult:** Rich doesn't understand about sharing yet. Could you please say, "Rich, I want my truck, but you can have this other toy" and gently trade with him?
> **Sam:** Rich, I want my truck, but you can have this other toy. Here!!

This will sometimes work, but certainly not all of the time. The point is to give the older sibling a tool—trading—rather than having them just grab the toy back or tell on their sibling. The baby stage does not last all that long, and once receptive language begins to kick in, you can begin to set expectations.

☺ ✎ PRESCHOOLER/EARLY-ELEMENTARY-AGE CHILDREN

Once a child begins to develop receptive language (page 114), he can begin to learn to take turns. One of the most effective fundamental scripting routines is for taking turns. Inevitably, when children are first learning language, they are also learning to take turns and share.

Initially, they are not very adept at either, so the language routine goes something as follows:

Sam grabs a toy from Sarah.
Adult: Sam, you may not grab. You can say, "Sarah, may I have a turn please?"
Sam: Sarah, may I have a turn please?
Sarah: No!
Adult: You may not say 'no,' but you may say, "You can have a turn in a minute" *(or, ". . . when I am through," or any number of reasonable comments).*
Sarah: You can have a turn in twenty-seven minutes *(kids can be wise guys).*
Adult: You need to be reasonable. How about three minutes? Say, "You can have a turn in three minutes."
Sarah: You can have a turn in three minutes.

Inevitably, after about a minute, Sarah will hand over the toy. Parents often underestimate a child's ability to take turns, and are shocked to see this kind of interaction work out so well. The two key reasons it all works out are *language* and *power*. Once a child is given the control to determine (within appropriate limits) when she hands over the toy, and she has the words to communicate that, then she is happy to do so. Conversely, once a child understands that she is next in line

> *It is when an adult forces an issue immediately that kids feel powerless and angry.*

and will be given a turn in a reasonable time, she can be patient. It is when an adult forces an issue immediately that kids feel powerless and angry (and in many ways, this is an appropriate reaction for them).

This routine takes: *practice, practice, and more practice.* Taking turns is hard; using the appropriate language is hard; but it does work with patience and practice. This same routine can be used for many situations, from sharing blocks to sharing video game time. *Whatever is being shared, the routine is the same: 1) ask for a turn; and 2) establish a reasonable time period for the turn.*

If the child does not give up the object in question after a few minutes, the follow-up can go something like this:

> *Adult:* Sarah, it has been about three minutes. Could you please give Sam the toy and say, "Here you go; it is your turn."
>
> *Sarah:* Here you go, it is your turn.
>
> *Adult:* Sam, can you say, "Thank you."
>
> *Sam:* Thank you.

When using a scripting technique for conflict resolution, the adult usually needs to literally provide the conversation for both sides. Remember here that the scripts need to be given *in child language.* For example, if a child knocks over another child's block structure, you could use adult language to correct the situation, using words like, "Friends don't knock each other's blocks over." However, the resolution will go much better if you offer a script couched in child language, such as:

> *Adult:* Say, "Please don't knock over my blocks!!!"
>
> *Child:* Please don't knock over my blocks!

Very often, annoying behavior at this age stems from a child feeling left out. They want to be included, but they don't know how to ask, so they do what they know will get them attention. If you point it out and give them alternate strategies, they will try them! Here is an example of a conflict-resolution script for a preschooler who is seeking attention:

> *Sarah:* Mom, Stefan is singing 'My Little Pony is skinny and bony!' *(a song that Stefan knows bothers her because My Little Ponies are her favorite toys).*
>
> *Adult:* What did you say to him?
>
> *Sarah:* Nothing.
>
> *Adult:* Can you tell him, "Stefan, please stop singing that song."
>
> *Sarah:* Stefan, can you please stop singing that song?
>
> *Adult:* Stefan, I think you are probably feeling left out. Can you say, "Okay, Sarah, I will stop singing, but can you let me play with you?"
>
> *Stefan:* Okay, Sarah, I will stop singing, but can you let me play with you?
>
> *Sarah:* Okay. You can be Starsong.

Here's another common scenario with a child who wants to be a part of the action:

> *Bob:* Mom, Jill keeps coming into my room and bugging me.
>
> *Adult:* What were you doing?
>
> *Bob:* Playing with Legos.
>
> *Adult:* Why do you think she was bugging you?
>
> *Bob:* I don't know.
>
> *Adult:* Do you think maybe she wants to play Legos?
>
> *Bob:* Maybe.
>
> *Adult:* Do you want to play Legos with Bob?

Jill: Yes.

Adult: Jill, can you say, "Bob, can I play Legos with you?"

Jill: Bob, Can I play Legos with you?

Bob: No!!

Adult: Bob, can you say, "I am in the middle of building a set right now; can you bring in another toy, and I will play with you as soon as this part is done."

Bob: I am in the middle of building a set right now! Can you bring in another toy, and I will play with you as soon as this part is done.

Very often, it is a matter of us using our experienced, logical brain to come up with alternate solutions. Kids see things in black-and-white. They see 'his way' or 'my way.' It helps immeasurably to present a creative solution to the current conflict—or better, help them to draw a creative solution through scaffolding different options. For example:

Sam: Donna said she won't play with me.

Donna: He is so annoying!

Adult: Donna, what are you playing?

Donna: A video game.

Adult: Did you say that you wouldn't play with Sam?

Donna: Yes.

Adult: Why?

Donna: Because I want to play Mario Brothers, and he wants to play Asteroids.

Adult: So you both want to play different games. How do you think we can settle this? You could each take turns, you could decide to play a different game altogether if

you can't agree on either one, or you can agree to play
one today and one tomorrow. Which do you want to do?

Donna: Play Mario Brothers today and Asteroids tomorrow.

Adult: Can you ask your brother nicely, "Sam, can we
please play Mario Brothers today, and I will play Asteroids with you tomorrow?"

Donna: Sam, can we please play Mario Brothers today, and
I will play Asteroids with you tomorrow?

Again, this is scaffolding. We want to teach them that there are
alternate solutions, and then
eventually, we want to help
them to generate their own
options. With a bit of help,
kids can be quite reasonable
with one another and can
sometimes even find solutions
that we might not. Often, kids
have trouble because they feel

> *We want to teach them that there are alternate solutions, and then eventually, we want to help them to generate their own options.*

like they are not being respected. Once respect is given, they are willing to compromise.

✎ LATER ELEMENTARY-SCHOOL-AGE CHILDREN

Third grade is typically when kids start to have sleepovers, and also
when they stop inviting the whole class to a birthday party. Third
grade is when kids are more likely to form cliques that purpose-
fully exclude.

Most times, kids are not really trying to be mean when they exclude,
but they do not have the strategies to handle social situations well.

When kids exclude at this age, there are usually three main reasons: 1) they want to include someone but honestly don't know how; 2) they really want some special time together, and do not want to include anyone else in that special time; and 3) they are testing out "excluding" someone. Whatever their reasoning may be, it sets the stage: *third grade is when social issues begin to become problems.*

Usually, when adults see a child being excluded, the automatic reaction is to fix it with an adult direction: "Sam and Ted, stop leaving Bobby out. You need to let him play." This is counterproductive for two reasons. First, it does not give kids the strategies to work it out independently, and second, the power and status is with the adult, leaving Bobby with even less status than before. Instead, take time to script the situation.

Since we already covered strategies for inclusion in Chapter Ten, let's focus right now on the second reason for exclusion: they really want some "special time" together, and do not want to include anyone else in that "special time." Here's some scripting language you can use:

Sarah: Mom, Jenna and Rosie said I can't play with them.
Adult: What did you say to them?
Sarah (in a very whiney tone): I said, "I want to play."
Adult: That tone is very whiney. Can you say, "Jenna and Rosie, I want to play with you. Please let me play."
Jenna: But Mom, why can't Rosie and I play alone? We have been playing with Sarah all afternoon!
Adult: Instead of saying that she can't play with you, can you say, "Sarah, can Rosie and I play for ten minutes on our own, and then we will do something with you?"

Jenna: Sarah, can Rosie and I play for ten minutes on our own, and them we will do something with you?
Sarah: Okay.

Here is an example of scripting after an event that involves exclusion takes place:

Judy: Sue was being mean to me at school today!
Mom: How was she being mean?
Judy: She wouldn't let me play with her.
Mom: Was she playing alone or with someone else?
Judy: She was playing with Ellie.
Mom: What were they playing?
Judy: They were drawing.
Mom: Were they working on a picture together?
Judy: Yes.
Mom: Maybe next time you could say, "Hey guys, can I draw with you when you are done with this picture?" Or maybe they wanted to have some time together that was just the two of them. Maybe you could say, "Hey guys, when you are done drawing, can we all do something together?"

Sometimes, it takes a lot of negotiating on our part to try to find out what a child should be saying. And here's one scenario that many of us face as parents all the time, when it is hard to draw our children out and find out exactly what is wrong:

> *Sometimes, it takes a lot of negotiating on our part to try to find out what a child should be saying.*

Adult: Jan, what's up today? You seem a little bit down.

Jan: Nothing . . . .

Adult: How was school today?

Jan: Fine.

Adult: Who did you sit with at lunch?

Jan: Sally and Lydia.

Adult: Did you sit with them in the classroom?

Jan: No, they never include me! When we got to the classroom, they went and sat at a table with no more chairs, and they left me out. I had to go over to sit next to Adam. The two of them were laughing the whole time in class. They were probably laughing at me!

Adult: That sounds like it was really hard. Do you think they meant to leave you out?

Jan: Yes! No! Oh, I don't know! They are so mean! I hate them.

Adult: Did you say anything to them?

Jan: Like what? "You guys are mean, and I never want to be your friend?"

Adult: No, something like, "Hey guys, can we move over to that other table so that I can sit with you too?"

Jan: No, but they probably would have said "no" anyway.

Adult: They might have, but they might have been happy to move. When stuff like that happens, sometimes people are doing things without thinking really about them, so you need to speak up and say what you want. If they say "no," it might be that they have something that they want to do on their own for a little while. That doesn't mean that they don't like you or they are being mean. Just say, "Hey guys, can we do something together later?" and give them some space to be together.

PRETEENS/ TEENS

When dealing with preteens and teens, it is really important to keep in mind they are experiencing hormonal changes. Hormones happen—and they can begin to have an effect as early as eight years of age in girls!

When hormones begin to be released, it really can cause some emotional havoc. We need to recognize that these changes are real, confusing, and difficult for them. *They have feelings that they don't understand, and sometimes this causes them to be irrational.* This is a time period when tweens and teens need limits more than ever. They also need to know that we understand what they are going through, but that does not give them a right to treat their family or friends poorly.

> *When hormones begin to be released, it really can cause some emotional havoc. We need to recognize that these changes are real, confusing, and difficult for them.*

When dealing with preteens and teenagers, we can easily minimize the importance of something in their lives, which can be one of our greatest pitfalls. To us, it may seem like they are being overdramatic, but to them (particularly girls), every minute of every day is the most important thing that has ever happened to them in their lives. Think about how exhausting that must be! We need to give them perspective, but we also need to recognize that

> It is our job to scaffold perspective.

they do not have it yet. It is our job to *scaffold perspective.* Here's an example of how we can help teens and preteens negotiate a conflict that is driving them crazy:

Ned: Bill is such a jerk!!

Adult: What happened, honey?

Ned (throwing his keys across the kitchen counter): Bill's such an ass!

Adult: I can see you are angry, but it doesn't give you a right to yell at me or to throw your keys like that. Why don't you sit down and read the comics for a minute, or have a bite to eat, and then we can talk about it?

Adult (a few minutes later): Okay—are you ready to talk?

Ned: Yeah.

Adult: What happened?

Ned: At lunch today I was sitting with Bill and Todd, and we were talking about the game last Saturday. Gina came over and sat at the table behind us, and Bill threw my hat and it landed at the other table, spilling soda all over Gina. Then Bill told her that I did it on purpose so that I could clean her shirt!! I was so embarrassed! Everyone was staring at me, and Gina gave me the dirtiest look. I can't believe he did that to me.

Adult: Yeah, I can understand why you are mad. Why do you think he said that?

Ned: Because he's a jerk.

Adult: Okay, but why do you really think he said it?

Ned: Because he has a crush on Gina, and he was embarrassed by what happened.

Adult: That sounds like a good guess. What do you think you want to do?

Ned: Nothing.

Adult: I don't know about that. If you are that angry and Bill embarrassed you that much, I think it is important for you to let him know.

Ned: It won't change anything. He's not going to tell her that he lied.

Adult: Okay—maybe he won't, but isn't it important to stick up for yourself and let him know that you don't want to be treated that way?

Ned: Yeah, I guess.

Adult: Do you think that tomorrow you could say to him, "I know why you told Gina that I threw the hat, but that's just not cool. I didn't tell her that you are the one with the crush on her because we are friends, so don't do that to me again."

Ned: Yeah, I guess.

So much of conflict negotiation with teens is about figuring out how they can save face, but still be able to stick up for themselves. Fortunately, if they learn how to, it's a skill that will serve them well as they get older.

Stage 3- CRAFTING THE APOLOGY

The last stage of conflict resolution is crafting the apology. Seems like it should be the easiest but it may be the toughest.

We want kids to apologize and move on. Sometimes they won't. This can be hard for us to understand, because we often underestimate their feelings. Think about how you deal with apologies. Can you apologize easily and move on? Do you apologize genuinely and own the behavior that hurt someone else? Adults may struggle with apologizing and we need to remember it's the same for kids.

Apologizing is a very important social skill, and if a child has done something worthy of an apology, he or she should apologize. Apologies are powerful and can diffuse many situations. But there are two types of apologies, and it is important to understand the distinction between them.

The first type is when there is *a simple and unintentional mistake,* such as one child accidentally bumping into another. Once kids understand that saying "I am sorry" is not an indication of intention and it does not mean that they did something wrong, they are usually pretty quick to apologize. Adults might explain that in an accident, "I'm sorry" really means, "I didn't mean to do it." Apologies of this type avoid hard feelings, and it is really useful for children to get used to making them. Here is a script for that:

> *There are two types of apologies, and it is important to understand the distinction between them.*

> *Marco:* Sarah kicked me!
>
> *Sarah:* I didn't mean to! I didn't see him there!
>
> *Adult:* Sarah, I understand it was an accident. Can you say, "Marco, I'm sorry I kicked you by mistake. I didn't see you there."
>
> *Sarah:* Marco, I'm sorry I kicked you by mistake. I didn't see you there.

Make them repeat their apology if it is given in an inappropriate tone, such as a begrudging or not-sincere-sounding one. The effect that an apology has when it is given correctly is very powerful, and in most cases, once an apology is given, all the kids are ready to move on. If a child really gets hurt, it may take a bit longer before he is ready to accept the apology, but if it was really unintentional, he will accept it reasonably quickly.

> *If the child does not willingly apologize, or the victim does not believe that it was unintentional, there is usually something going on, and they need help to work it out.*

Occasionally, the victim cannot believe that it was unintentional. In these cases, it requires a bit more follow-up and scripting, and it should be treated as the second type of apology: *when someone has intentionally done something to hurt someone else.*

If a child does not willingly apologize, or the victim does not believe that it was unintentional, there is usually something more going on, and they need help to work it out. This is the perfect situation for scripting! *Through scripting, adults can find out what happened and why each person is upset, and then craft an effective apology that provides for the taking of responsibility for certain actions, but also allows for children to state their justification as well.* Situations are very rarely one-sided, and sometimes it may be appropriate for both sides to give an apology. Here is an example:

Jenna (crying): Mom, Marco kicked me and I fell off the chair, and I hit my head on the table.
Adult: Marco, did you kick her?
Marco: Yeah, but she kept bugging me when I was trying

to read! I kept telling her to go away and she didn't listen, so finally I got frustrated and kicked her.

Adult: Marco, can you say, "Jenna, I am sorry that I kicked you and you got hurt, but when I ask you to stop bugging me when I am reading, please listen to what I am saying."

Marco: Jenna, I am sorry that I kicked you and you got hurt, but when I ask you to stop bugging me when I am reading, please listen to what I am saying.

Adult: Jenna, can you say, "Okay, Marco, I am sorry that I kept bugging you, but please don't kick me."

Jenna: Marco, I am sorry that I kept bugging you, but please don't kick me.

Now for a situation that is a bit less straightforward: sometimes, you will find that the event was started by an underlying anger that has been festering for a while, so it takes a bit of work to figure out what is going on. Let's look at an example:

Carli: I am so mad at Sheila! She posted a picture of me on Facebook that I told her not to. She is such a jerk.

Adult: Okay, but you and Sheila have been friends for a long time, and that doesn't sound like something that she would usually do. So let's find out why she did it. I understand that you are angry, but did something happen before she posted the picture?

Carli: I don't know!

Adult: Have the two of you been hanging out lately?

Carli: Not much. I have been hanging out with Debbie.

Adult: Who has Sheila been hanging out with?

Carli: I don't know.

Adult: Has she tried to hang out with you and Debbie?

Carli: Yeah, but we want to have some time alone.

Adult: Have you talked to Sheila about that?

Carli: No.

Adult: How do you think that makes her feel?

Carli: I don't know. Bad, I guess.

Adult: You know, you and Sheila have been friends for a long time. I bet she is feeling pretty bad about being left out. You might want to give her a call and tell her that you are upset that she posted the picture on Facebook, but you understand that you haven't been treating her very well. Maybe you can see if she wants to come over this weekend so you can spend some time together.

Carli: Yeah, I guess so.

The important part is to craft an apology that each side feels comfortable with. Children are rarely able to do this on their own until they have had practice, so it takes an adult to act as a referee, scaffolding the interaction and providing the children with the words that they need.

It's a Win-Win!

Scripting can help you successfully negotiate almost any contentious interaction.

Scripting can help you successfully negotiate almost any contentious interaction. Children really appreciate the scaffolding from adults, because they are being given the language to work out a conflict they often don't know how to resolve themselves.

Scripting doesn't always work because we do not live in an ideal or perfect world! But it does work most times, *if* you find a successful "win" for both parties by giving them the scripted language they can use. It teaches children the early skill of negotiation, and gives them the feeling that both parties can compromise and still come out ahead.

PART FOUR

The Plan: Proactive Parenting

→

Chapter Twelve

◆ ◆ ◆

The Plan:
Be Prepared!

The Boy Scouts have it right: we need to be prepared! Parents must prepare children to handle situations, so that they may be resilient. That is why our parenting needs to be *proactive*.

Throughout this book, we have made the point that through our everyday parenting moments, we can teach our children resilience. We have outlined the Four Ss as the framework for teaching in those moments, and we have presented scripting as a tool that can help teach those Four Ss in everyday challenges.

The first two sections of the book primarily deal with "ideal" scripting—the way that scripting can work in a perfect world. We offered it that way because it makes understanding the process of scripting easier for you. But as we just pointed out, *we all know that we don't live in that "perfect" world.*

Proactive parenting is about having *a plan in place* to avoid control battles. When we are prepared to handle emotion and the need for control, we can access the Four Ss. The lessons that our kids learn prepare them to be resilient in many circumstances. By being proactive parents, we have taken advantage of an opportunity to use upcoming situations of crisis to our—and our children's—advantage!

Conflict happens. There is no getting around it. There will be times when we disagree with others. There is conflict within families, between friends, and within marriages. It is natural. However, conflict does not necessarily need to turn into *crisis*. Conflict is challenging, but parents as well as children can learn how to negotiate it successfully.

Proactive parenting is about having a plan in place to avoid control battles.

The plan that we set out for handling emotional conflict is proactive, allowing parents to step back and make decisions about limits with less of the emotional charge that can hijack our brains. With a plan in place, conflicts become *teachable moments*.

The Resilience Formula is a plan that can be used in many instances: battles of control between parents and their children, fights between siblings, even marital arguments—any time that emotion gets in the way of communication. The idea is *to have a plan in place that allows everyone to calm down and negotiate an appropriate solution.*

The plan has three stages: 1) before the conflict, 2) during the conflict, and 3) after the conflict.

Stage 1- BEFORE THE CONFLICT

Being proactive requires preparation, so the plan needs to be in place before conflict takes place in order for it to be effective. Often, a plan is set in place *in reaction to* crisis. Instead, have a plan in place before you even need it.

Here are the guidelines to follow before your child is in crisis:

1- UNDERSTAND THE RULES. In *7 Things Your Teenager Won't Tell You And How to Talk About Them Anyway*, the authors suggest having three rules for teens: 1) be respectful, 2) stay in touch, and 3) stay safe. For younger children, the rules can probably be limited to be respectful and stay safe—although we would also add, "stay healthy."

> *With a plan in place, control battles become teachable moments.*

Having these simple rules in place allows parents to frame conflicts in very simple terms. When a conflict begins, rely on the rules as a framework for a triggerscript.

Here is an example:
Adult: No, you can't have another cookie.
Child: Pleeease?
Adult: No, we are having dinner shortly, and I want you to eat dinner to stay healthy.

The use of "stay healthy" triggers a reaction in the child—for the child knows already, *this is one of the rules in my house.* The reaction that they have determines the next step a parent should take. In the basic scripting, we talked about scripting appropriate replies (see Chapter Nine), but what happens if the appropriate replies do not work? What happens when children start getting rude? Get angry? Start to cry? That is when it is great to have a plan in place!

2- CHOOSE A SAFE SPACE FOR A COOLING-OFF PERIOD. Remember, when kids get out of control, they do things that they regret. Often, they can be destructive, to property or relationships. They say things that they don't mean and afterward, they feel horrible. They need a place to escape before they are destructive. Ironically, teens often naturally try to get away to avoid this, but most adults stop them with, "Don't walk away when I am speaking to you!" That reveals an adult's need for control, one that unfortunately leads to destructive and counterproductive responses from their children. Instead, encourage children to go away to a safe and comforting spot, one where they begin realizing that in the end, the problem can be worked out without all the emotion!

The space for a cooling-off period is a place that kids can go to calm down—a "time-out" spot, if you will. It's not a punishment place; that's not the point. We like to use the word "cool down" spot so it is clear – this isn't punishment- just a place to cool down so we can talk. It is for a child (or anyone) to take a break, calm down, and get it together so that they are ready to resolve the conflict—whatever type of conflict it might be. *How long should the "cool down" be?* As long as it takes—sometimes a few seconds, sometimes a few minutes, sometimes longer. The "cool down" is done or over *when the person is calm and ready to talk reasonably.* If we want to teach resilience, we need to teach kids that they can have control to decide when they are ready, but we need to give them the tools they need to do it successfully. The goal here is to give them a safe place to escape and avoid the threatening situation.

3- SELECT A TRIGGERSCRIPT that sends them to the spot. It can be as simple as, "Go sit on the steps," or "Change tracks!" As kids get older, let them help to determine the spot as well as the triggerscript. Because the triggerscript is agreed upon ahead of time, it should trigger your child (or you!) to be able to walk away.

4- DECIDE ON THE BOUNDARIES during the cooling-off period. Once a child has been triggered to walk away to her space, she needs to have an understanding of what the expectations are while she is there. *Everyone needs to be clear about the limits.*

For younger kids, the cooling-off period is likely to be pretty short—usually just a few minutes. Therefore, the expectations are somewhat straightforward, but there are a few things that need to be clear and agreed upon. You might need to clarify things such as the following: Can your child go to the bathroom? If he has a "safety object" (blanket, stuffed toy, etc), can he get it to bring to the spot? Are there activities that your child can do to help calm down, like coloring or reading? The thing to keep in mind is that this is not a punishment—it is a time to cool down.

For older kids, it becomes more complex, particularly because a cooling-off period may be much longer. The limits for that period need to be clear. Some examples of appropriate limits are: no taking or making of phone calls or texts during this period. Whatever limits you decide, make sure that you listen if your kids have a good argument for a limit that should not be set. For example, if music calms your child, it may not make sense to take away the iPod when they are calming down.

Again, the cooling-off period is not a time for punishment—consequences for inappropriate behaviors come later. This is a difficult concept for many parents: in the emotional moment, when our children have hurt us or threatened our authority, we do not want them to be

> *The cooling-off period is not a time for punishment.*

"rewarded" in any way—and this is how some parents view the place of safety. However, we need to keep in mind that what is best is to help our kids calm down when they are out of control. Some kids may need to get rid of their energy, and if your child is one of those kids, let them go to a place where they can blow off steam safely. Set the limits ahead of time, and have a plan that makes sense for your child—not one that fuels your own need for control. Remember when you are setting limits, that young kids will have a cooling-off period that will probably not be very long (usually only a few minutes), but it might take days before your teen is really ready to talk. For older kids, make limits that can last for a few days.

> *Set the limits ahead of time, and have a plan that makes sense for your child—not one that fuels your own need for control.*

5- CREATE A "READY SCRIPT" for when everyone is ready. To us, it may seem obvious that our children will let us know when they are ready, but their reality is different. Why? They may be feeling embarrassed about their actions, and do not know how to reach out. So again: the best thing to do is to script it for them.

The script needs to be simple, such as, "Mom, I am ready to talk." The tone of the script becomes important, too, in recognizing when they are, in fact, ready to talk. The reason that we set the script beforehand is that it will be difficult for our kids to hear it during the actual conflict. It will be easier for them to be able to say the script if they know it ahead of time.

Stage 2- During the Conflict

1- SAY THE TRIGGERSCRIPT. Though this may seem easy, it is not. It is often difficult for us to recognize the need for calm-down time when we are in the moment. We find ourselves engaging in control battles without remembering there is a way out! With practice, however, it gets easier. It is a matter of stopping to say the triggerscript and walking away.

Here is an example:

> **Adult:** "David, go to the steps to cool down. When you are ready to come back and work this out, say, "Mom, I'm ready."

Once you have said the triggerscript, you need to WAIT. *Move away, and give them time!*

Sometimes, even as parents, we need someone to tell us to step away. Planning a trigger ahead of time can be helpful for us too. Here's a story to illustrate this.

One day, Donna's daughter said, "Mom, sometimes you turn into Azula when you are angry!" Donna got her daughter's meaning

> *Once you have said the triggerscript, you need to WAIT. Move away, and give them time!*

right away: Azula is a character in their favorite series, *The Last Airbender.* She is the evil character. Donna was struck by this comment, and she didn't want that association. So she told her daughter that whenever she saw Azula coming out of her, she should say, "Mom, you are turning into Azula; please take time out." The next time Donna was angry, her daughter said the script—and Donna walked away. The script was the trigger! As soon as Donna heard the name "Azula," she moved away and took the time she needed to get under control.

We need triggers to get us out of danger. The idea of the plan is to create a triggerscript that triggers a reaction—a reaction that is scheduled and predictable in order to keep everyone safe—until we are ready to have a reasonable discussion.

2- MOVE AWAY. The mention of a cool-down spot is often a time that emotional kids bait adults into another control battle. An enraged toddler may holler out "NOOOO!!!" when told to go to the steps. A teen may scream back, "*I hate you! I'm never going to be ready to talk to you.*" Our instinct is to scream back; *don't.* As long as your children are not doing anything danger-ous, *move away to avoid the battle.* First, repeat that you expect them to go to the cool down spot to calm and that you will know they are 'ready' once they have met your expectation of a calmly-uttered 'ready' script. *Then move away and wait until they do.*

When children offer up a challenge as their response, one of the most important things we must do is NOT ENGAGE. As the parent, you may need a cool down spot, too. The scripts and plan we offer in this book can be used both for your kids *and yourself.* If and when they are used for you, it teaches positive and appro-priate role modeling to your children.

When your child emerges to say the "ready-script," make sure that they really are ready. If they scream "MOM, I'M READY!!!!," restate the expectation: "I hear you saying that you are ready, but I will know that you are ready to talk when you can say it calmly, as in 'Mom, I am ready to talk.'" Then give them space again until they say it appropriately. If your kids come back before they are truly ready, the conflict is only likely to start all over again.

By setting the expectation for children, adults give them the power to decide when they are ready. Likely, they will not say the script correctly until they are, in fact, ready. Occasionally, they will be ready before you are. If that happens, it is fine to say, "I am still too angry to talk. I will let you know when I am ready."

Stage 3- AFTER THE CONFLICT

1- SCRIPT THE CONVERSATION. Once everyone involved is ready to talk, it is time to discuss *what happened*. This is when scripting comes into play again. Communication is difficult, but communicating when we have disappointed someone we love is especially hard.

Think back to the last argument you had with someone that you cared about—a spouse, your mother, a good friend. Even as adults, most of us have trouble knowing what to say, how to apologize, or how to voice our needs. Think how much easier it would be to have someone help out with the script!

> *Scripting is the process of questioning, drawing out answers, and then scripting back what they can say.*

Sometimes, it is too difficult for children to express how they felt or what they need. Scripting is *the process of questioning, drawing out answers, and then scripting back what they can say.* In order to do this, it is important to listen to what children are saying, even if it seems irrational. We can listen, acknowledge what they feel, and try to frame it in a way that everyone's needs are met. Keep in mind that their feelings may not always seem rational, but they are real—so we need to help them deal with them appropriately. If your child is having trouble telling you why he is upset, give him the opportunity to write down his feelings—and use that as a basis of the script.

If the scripting is not working, or your child is refusing to speak to you, explain calmly that there are certain restrictions on his behavior until the matter is resolved (which puts you back to the "cooling-off" period). Those restrictions may have been part of the plan, or you can negotiate them if you are both in a state of reasonable emotions. Remember, however, that the adult needs to be the one to set the guidelines and restrictions and stick to them. Once again, give your child a script for what to say when he or she is ready to resolve the issue (e.g., "Mom, I am ready to talk now.") When he is ready, he has the opportunity to come to you; however, for some kids it is helpful to check in every once in a while ("Are you ready to resolve that issue yet?").

In the follow-up, make sure that you express your own feelings rationally. If there is something that you said or did that you regret, take responsibility for it and apologize. Ask your child if there is anything he needs you to say. If it is something that you are not willing to say (such as granting them permission to use the car tonight), explain why that is not going to happen.

2- SET THE CONSEQUENCES. Once the conflict has been discussed, set the consequences for their earlier actions. Particularly in instances when kids have been destructive, they need consequences that will help them heal. They need to make amends because they feel badly about what they have done—so go ahead, give them that opportunity! Make sure you are calm when you do so, because typically, when we are emotional, we tend to throw out extreme consequences. If we wait until we are calm, however, we are able to have a discussion and decide on something reasonable. Once the consequence has been set, be prepared to follow through on making sure they do it.

The most important thing to remember is that children *need unconditional love and support.* They need to know that while you did not like their behavior and you became angry about it, you still love them and are proud of them. Continue to show that you love them—*they need it even more when they have done something wrong.*

> **Children need unconditional love and support.**

3- USE THE TEACHABLE MOMENT! Once the issue has been resolved, there is an opportunity to make it a teachable moment. Discuss what has been learned with your child, using the Four Ss as a guideline. The goal is to teach resilience, and each resolved challenge is an opportunity to do that!

Traditionally, if there are control battles going on, our kids can learn these scary messages, which undermine their resilience:

- SELF: I can't control my emotions, and I do things I regret. I am no good. I have no power in this relationship.

- SITUATION: This situation was tragic. I lost respect from my parents. I never want to do this again.

- SUPPORT: My parents got angry at me. I don't like it when they are angry, so I won't go to them for help.

- ◆ STRATEGIES: My only strategy is to scream, and it gets me in trouble.

But if we use the plan effectively, our kids can learn:

- ◆ SELF: With some support, I can calm myself down when I am upset, which avoids destructive behaviors.

- ◆ SITUATION: With help, I can handle this situation. I didn't like it, but it wasn't terrible.

- ◆ SUPPORT: My parents are there to support and love me, even when I am angry.

- ◆ STRATEGIES: I learned strategies to get myself out of trouble, and I can use them in the future in times of conflict.

So there it is . . . the Resilience Formula for proactive parenting during challenges. In essence, it is having a plan in place. Use trigger-scripts to control emotion. Script a solution that uses the Four Ss as a framework. *In this way, we build the foundation for resilience in our children to enable them to handle life's challenges, both big and small.*

The Plan: In Review

Stage 1: Before the Conflict

1- Understand the "rules."

2- Choose a safe space for a cool-off period.

3- Select a triggerscript to send them to the spot.

4- Decide on the boundaries during the cool-off time.

5- Create a "ready" script for when everyone is ready.

Stage 2: During the Conflict

1- Say the *triggerscript.*

2- Move away.

Stage 3: After the Conflict

1- *Script* the conversation.

2- Set the consequences.

3- Use the teachable moment.

Afterword

Parenting is a huge challenge. It can be extremely rewarding, but it is difficult along the way! We wish that we could give you a formula that is foolproof—"If you do this, parenting will be easy"—but we can't. Nobody can because the world is imperfect. We hope, however, that this book will make you comfortable trying out some new and effective ways to conduct yourself as parents. We hope you feel good about the lessons your children are learning so they can become independent adults themselves.

The strategies in this book do work, but like anything else, they need practice. As you learn to apply them even in the most challenging of situations, you will see your children learning the scripts that will help them manage their own lives. Most importantly, you will be planting the roots of resilience that will give your child the strength to handle greater challenges that present themselves in the future. And what a great thing that is for us to give our children.

—Donna M. Volpitta, Ed.D. and Joel D. Haber, Ph.D.

References & Suggested Readings

Ackerly, R. (2012). The genius in every child: Encouraging character, curiosity, and creativity in children. CT: Lyons, Press.

Barish, K. (2012). Pride and joy: A guide to understanding your child's emotions and solving family problems. NY: Oxford University Press.

Borba, M. (2002). Building moral intelligence: The seven essential virtues that teach kids to do the right thing. CA: Jossey-Bass.

Brooks, R & Goldstein, S. (2004). The power of resilience: Achieving balance, confidence, and personal strength in your life. NY, NY: McGraw Hill.

Evans, R. (2004). Family matters: How schools can cope with the crisis in childrearing. San Francisco, CA: Jossey-Bass.

Faber, A. & Mazlish E. (1980). How to talk so your kids will listen & listen so your kids will talk. NY: Harper.

Geidd, J. (2011). Development of the young brain. May 2, 2011 National Institute of Mental Health.
http://www.nimh.nih.gov/news/media/video/giedd.shtml

Ginsburg, K. (2006) A Parent's guide to building resilience in children and teens: Giving your child roots and wings. American Academy of Pediatrics.

Gottlieb, L. (2011 July/ August). How to land your kid in therapy. The Atlantic, www.theatlantic.com/magazine/archive/2011/07/how-to-land-your-kid-in-therapy/8555/

Hallowell, E.M. (1997). Worry. NY: Pantheon Books.

Haber, J and Glatzer, J (2007) Bullyproof your child for life: Protect your child from teasing, taunting and bullying for good. NY, NY Penguin/Perigee.

Lippincott, J.M. & Deutsch, R.M (2005). 7 things your teenager won't tell you and how to talk about them anyway. NY: Ballentine Books.

Mogel, W. (2008). The blessings of a skinned knee: Using jewish teachings to raise self-reliant children. NY; Penguin Putnam Inc.

Reid, D. K. (1998). Scaffolding: A broader view. Journal of Learning Disabilities, 31(4), 386–396.

Reivich, K. & Shatte, A. (2002). The resilience factor: 7 essential skills for overcoming life's obstacles. NY: Broadway Books.

Rutter, M. (2006). Implications of resilience concepts for scientific understanding. Annals of the New York Academy of Sciences, 1094, 1–12.

Schley, B. (2010). The Microscripting Rules: It's not what people hear. It's what they repeat.... NY: N.W. Widener.

Schurgin O'Keefe, G.(2011). CyberSafe: Protecting and empowering kids in the digital world of texting, gaming, and social media. American Academy of Pediatrics.

Shure, M.B. (2005). Thinking parent, thinking child. NY: McGraw Hill.

Seligman, M.E. (1998). Learned optimism: How to change your mind and your life. Pocket Books.

Siegel, D. J. & Payne Bryson, T. (2012). The whole-brain child: 12 revolutionary strategies to nurture your child's developing mind. NY: Bantam Books.

Siegel, D. (2012). Pocket guide to interpersonal neurobiology. NY: Mind Your Brain, Inc.

Siegel, D. (2009). The power of mindsight. TEDx talk. www.youtube.com/watch?v=Nu7wEr8AnHw

Tierney, J. (July 18, 2011). Can a playground be too safe? The New York Times. http://www.nytimes.com/2011/07/19/science/19tierney.html

Tool Kits for Kids. www.toolkitsforkids.com

Van Tassell, Gene. http://www.brains.org/path.htm

Waddell, C. www.one-revolution.org

Young-Eisendrath, P. (2008) The self-esteem trap: Raising confident and compassionate kids in an age of self-importance. NY, NY: Little, Brown, & Co.

Please visit our websites for an updated list of references:

Haber, J. **www.respectu.com**

Volpitta, D. **www.URresilient.com**

About the Authors

DONNA VOLPITTA, Ed.D., is an educator who is passionate about the field of resilience. Through her workshops and education programs, she offers practical strategies to teach resilience and integrity.

Dr. Volpitta is a board member of the One Revolution Foundation (www.one-revolution.org) and she helped create Nametags, One Revolution's outreach education program. Dr. Volpitta is also an education advisor for Kids Helping Kids (www.kidshelpingkidsct.org) a non-profit organization dedicated to developing leaders through youth-led service projects. She writes an education blog for www.modernmom.com, has authored several articles, received a grant from the Department of Education, and has given presentations at numerous professional conferences.

Dr. Volpitta is a former classroom teacher with experience in both general and special education. She holds a doctoral degree in Learning Dis/Abilities from Teachers College, Columbia University and lives in New York with her husband and four children.

To find out more or contact Dr. Volpitta, please visit her website at www.URresilient.com.

Dr. JOEL HABER is the author of the internationally acclaimed, *"Bullyproof Your Child for Life: Protect Your Child from Teasing, Taunting and Bullying for Good"* published by Perigee/Penguin. Dr. Haber is a Clinical Psychologist and nationally recognized parenting expert. He was selected as a webinar leader and a speaker for the Obama Administration Federal Partners in Bullying Prevention initiative. He is a leading authority for the LG Text Education Council, an advisory council, assembled by LG Mobile Phones (**www.LGTextEd.com**). The council members provide useful information on a variety of subjects and offer guidance to effectively handle issues concerning cyberbullying and mobile phone misuse. He is also an advisor to Cartoon Network's *STOP BULLYING: SPEAK UP* Campaign, which launched in 2010. In 2011, he became an expert contributor to ivillage.com. He is also an expert to *"No Snap Judgments"*, a national campaign to promote acceptance and tolerance amongst our youth, developed along with the **Addams Family** Broadway show.

The official bullying consultant to the American Camp Association, Dr. Haber helped write the standards for bully prevention and safety for all accredited summer camps under ACA. Dr. Haber provides on-site training for campers and staff, web-based material, educational courses, scholarly articles and research to the organization. He is also co-founder of Tool Kits for Kids **www.toolkitsforkids.com**, recipient of five national parenting awards for their emotional first aid kits, helping parents and kids develop tools and emotional life skills to overcome worry, build confidence and develop resilience.

He is an advisor to the new movie, "Bully" and an expert contributor to KIDS IN THE HOUSE, an online parenting video resource launching in 2012.

As founder of the Respect U Program, a bully prevention and management program used in schools, camps, organizations, sports teams and families; Dr. Haber has worked to improve the lives and social competencies of thousands of children and adults. Dr. Haber has published numerous comprehensive research studies of bullying and cyber bullying for schools and summer camps.

The author of numerous publications, he has been featured in a front-page article on bullying in the New York Times, on ABC, CBS National News and on ESPN and NPR radio. He has appeared in hundreds of newspaper and magazine articles.

For more information about Dr. Haber and his work, please visit www.respectu.com.

CPSIA information can be obtained at www.ICGtesting.com
Printed in the USA
BVOW02s1311091213

338601BV00001B/14/P

9 780985 236502